Communicating in science: writing and speaking

Communicating in science: writing and speaking

VERNON BOOTH

Trinity College, Cambridge

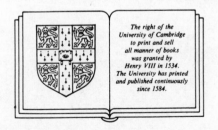

*The right of the
University of Cambridge
to print and sell
all manner of books
was granted by
Henry VIII in 1534.
The University has printed
and published continuously
since 1584.*

CAMBRIDGE UNIVERSITY PRESS

Cambridge

New York   Port Chester

Melbourne   Sydney

Published by the Press Syndicate of the University of Cambridge
The Pitt Building, Trumpington Street, Cambridge CB2 1RP
40 West 20th Street, New York, NY 10011, USA
10 Stamford Road, Oakleigh, Melbourne 3166, Australia

First published 1985
Reprinted 1985, 1987, 1988, 1990

Printed in Great Britain by the University Press, Cambridge

Library of Congress catalogue card number: 84–15537

British Library Cataloguing in Publication Data
Booth, Vernon
Communicating in science.
1. Technical writing
I. Title
808'.0665021 T11
ISBN 0 521 27771 X

Dedicated to Th. M'Fline

Contents

Balloons & marginal instructions

Words that appear in the margin and that are completely ringed ~~said~~ are said to be in a 'balloon'. If the balloon ~~has a~~ and a caret, the word or words go into the text. If there is no ~~tail~~, the balloon either contains clarification/blurred words, or it contains instructions that should not be typed or printed.

(margin: tail)

(margin: tail)

of

(margin: Dont type this)

Words in the margin (usually the left), bounded by one or two [ ], are instructions for ~~the printer~~. They should be typed. Instructions written on ~~the~~ typescript by hand and intended for ~~the~~ printer are best ringed.

(margin: Gk alpha])

(margin: [Fig 4 near here])

If you have crossed out a piece, then wish it kept, underline it with dots ~~and~~ write 'stet' in the margin. Stet means 'let it stand'.

(margin: stet)

(margin: NP) ~~There~~ is no guarantee given that all these conventions are ~~understood~~ world wide. Indicate that a new paragraph is needed as shown above.

(margin: NP)

If no new par is needed, draw a snake.

Preface

In one laboratory in Cambridge, if a person became unapproachable, we said he (she) was giving birth. Paper labour can be a traumatic experience, but should not be. The writing of a paper, or a book, although indeed a task, should be a pleasant occupation. Books on scientific writing have been published, but scientists 'do not have time' to read them. So, in 1970, I wrote an essay, *Writing a Scientific Paper* (i.e. *WASP*), and submitted it for a competition organized by Koch–Light Ltd; the essay was awarded first prize, and was subsequently issued as a booklet.

Later editions of *WASP* grew longer. For the present edition, various sections have been expanded into chapters. This makes the book longer than before, but the principal chapter remains short. This shortness has always been an important feature of *WASP*. The principal chapter keeps its original title but the book has a new title.

Chapters One and Three are intended primarily to help scientists and engineers to write papers for journals and to give short talks. However, nearly all the suggestions also apply to the writing of books and delivery of full lectures.

The style, especially of the first chapter, is succinct, at times even terse. So much had to be written, in so small a space, that conciseness was highly desirable. Chapter One is not suitable for fast reading.

Parts of the book are written in the imperative, the simplest style. This is not intended to be categorical. True, certain parts are controversial – but life would be dull if we all agreed. There may be errors; most books have errors. I am tempted to add (as an examinee once added) E. & O.E.[1]

Some of the words that are discussed are in 'quotes'. A plethora of quotes can be irritating; so, where the meaning should be clear without them, quotes are not used, even at the risk of some loss of consistency. Examples of a directive being discussed are referred to in brackets. Thus [p. 7 (13)] means there is an illustrative example or more information on

---

[1] Errors and omissions excepted.

p. 7 in the line marked in the margin by (13). B (0) refers to a number in the margin in Chapter Seven.

(1)   You will see M'Fline mentioned in various places. He is **The Man whose First Language Is Not English**. We must think all the time of him when we write or speak.

The majority of papers submitted for publication are returned to authors for revision. Without doubt, you would like each of your papers to be accepted without change. This book cannot guarantee your fulfilling that ambition, but perhaps it will help.

As you read this book, you may think that I enjoyed writing it. I offer best wishes that you too will enjoy writing, preparing scripts and speaking.

I am grateful to many, many colleagues, as well as to several editors in various countries, for help and suggestions.

Glossary of some printers' terms

balloon. Ring drawn round instructions to the printer. [P. viii.]

bold. Heavy type **as here**. In a script, underline with a wavy line.

braces. Curly brackets { }.

brackets. Square brackets [ ]. The term sometimes includes **parentheses, braces** and **angle brackets** ($\langle \rangle$).

caps, upper case. CAPITAL LETTERS. In a script underline thrice.

copy. The script. To avoid confusion, a **photocopy** should be so named.

em rule. Long dash (—). Length of cap M. [P. 19 (38).] Many publishers use a spaced en rule (–).

en rule. Short dash (–). Half the length of em rule.

foliation. Numbering of folios.

folio. (1) Sheet of script. (2) Page number. (3) Sheet of paper folded once.

full point. Full stop, period.

index. (1) Alphabetical list of topics at the end of a book. Plural, indexes. (2) See **superior** below.

inferior, subscript. Small low digit(s) or other character(s)$_{2n}$.

ital, italic. *Sloping type.* Spelt with l.c. 'i'. In a script, underline once.

leading. Space between lines of type. Pronounced 'ledding'.

l.c. Lower case. Small letters, i.e. not caps.

legend, caption. Explanation to a figure. Term sometimes also used for explanation to a table. Ideally, legends should be understandable without reference to the text, yet illogically, they are often set in smaller type. Legends (or captions) to figures are usually placed below, whereas those for tables are usually placed, more logically, above the display.

Science books published by Cambridge University Press are often more consistent, with the tables and figures placed at the foot of the page and the captions above them. This allows the text always to start at the top of a page and gives a more comfortable reading pattern.

numeral. Digit. See p. 14 under Homonyms.

par. Paragraph. [P. 28 (62).] **N.P.** New paragraph. [P. viii.] Indicate NP by □ or ⌐.

parens. Parentheses, round brackets ( ). [P. 20 (42).]

reference marks. * † ‡ § ‖ ¶ ** ††.... Use them in this order.

rom, roman. Normal upright type, not italic or bold. Spelt with l.c. 'r'.

run on. Continue in same par. See last sentence, p. viii.

sanserif, sans. Type without serifs. THIS is sans. H girder; O ring; S shape; T join; U tube; V groove. For text, sans is less legible than type with serifs. [B (1).] See The typewriter's type face, p. 31.

sm. cap, small caps. Capital-style letters only slightly larger than l.c. Used for EMPHASIS or for HEADINGS. In a script, underline twice.

superior, superscript. Small high digit(s) or other character(s)^{2n}. Also called **index**; plural, indices.

Chapter One
Writing a scientific paper

Before you write

(2) For your consideration I suggest four things you might do before you write a paper.

    1. In subjects in which notebooks are used, good notebook discipline is helpful. When an experiment is finished, try to record your conclusion in words together with your findings and on the same page. Make tables. Draw graphs and stick them into the book. Keep a separate book or file in which to record summaries of results from many experiments, and group them by subject. Some experiments will each provide results for various summaries.

    Prompt recording of summaries compels you to give critical thought to each experiment at the best time, and may move you to repeat a control test while you still have the materials. Clark (1960) makes an eloquent appeal for keeping adequate notes. Write every digit unmistakably. Say to yourself 'I must so write my notes that another person can read them if I am ill, or worse'. Then you should understand them yourself when you come to write the paper.

    2. Some institutes operate a regular tea club or occasional seminar at
(3) which research workers tell colleagues about their work. *Speaking makes you think out arguments*; and listeners' criticisms may prevent your publishing a clanger. If your institute has no club, or the programme is filled, invite colleagues to your room to listen to you. Display diagrams. If you have no projector, use a felt pen to draw diagrams and tables on the back of a roll of wallpaper. Hang the paper over a chair on the bench. Do – speak – slowly.

(4)   Nothing clarifies ideas in one's own mind so much as explaining them to other people.

    3. The third suggested pre-writing activity is based on Woodford's (1970) 'reservoirs'. Take 8 sheets of paper. Boldly label them

Title Summary Intro Mat Meth Results Disc Ref

Write ideas for your paper, whenever they come to you, as notes on the appropriate sheets. Use differently coloured sheets if possible. Carry a

1

card everywhere – even to bed. Jot down ideas as they occur. Transfer
the notes to the reservoirs and put a fresh card in your pocket. Rewrite
a cluttered reservoir from time to time; if you wait too long, you may
forget what some of your notes meant. Hold the reservoirs in a clothes
peg (pin), not in a wire clip which may 'steal' other papers.

  Some writers construct a skeleton, an outline scheme, before they
start to write. Should you do this it is still advisable first to prepare the
reservoirs. In particular, a skeleton for the Discussion may help you to
muster your ideas in the best order and to avoid repetition.

  4. Prepare tables and figures.

When to begin writing

My research supervisor said 'Writing a paper is as important as experiments. Is it unreasonable, then, if it takes as long?' Oft-repeated advice
is 'Set aside your paper for some weeks, then read it. You may be
amazed at what you wrote.' You may even discover a passage you yourself cannot understand. If you follow this advice, and believe that supervisor, you must start writing early. Writing as the work proceeds reveals
gaps in knowledge, gaps that should be filled while laboratory facilities
are still available.

Arrangement of a scientific paper

Although there is no standard arrangement for a scientific paper – and
people hope there never will be – the commonest arrangement is that
indicated by the titles of the reservoirs. Some investigations are suitable
for results and discussion to be written together in narrative form. If you
use this form, write your Conclusion as a separate section. If your
chosen journal issues an editorial directive that leaves you no choice,
you should arrange your paper accordingly.

Where to start

Even though you have enough material, you may have postponed
writing a projected paper. Perhaps you find it difficult to start. I do.
You do not have to begin with the Introduction. Begin with the easiest
section. This may be Methods, for you should know what you did. Use
the reservoirs, and cross out the notes as you consume them.

  Next, perhaps, you might start on the Results. Write the first draft 'in
your own words' just as though you are telling a friend about your
fascinating discoveries. Dont worry – yet – about grammar, aptest words
& style. The immediate objective is to get going. You can polish the

style later. This paragraph was so written, and the needless words and hackneyed phrases have not yet been polished out.

The Conclusion of a paper is so important that you should make its first draft in time to allow for re-draftings.

Stocktaking

Now take stock. The outline is complete, diagrams and tables are ready, the Discussion is planned, the Conclusion is drafted and Methods are written. Oh joy! the paper is half finished. A happy author writes better than a worried one.

Title and key words

Some searchers may read only the Title of the paper and the Summary. So both are supremely important parts of a paper. Compose trial
(7) versions of the title as early in your writing as you can; re-examine them later.

On your reservoir sheet write key words for the Title. Let the Title's first word be a key word if possible – in lists of titles such a word is better than 'The'. Remove other waste words such as 'on', 'study', 'investigation'.... The Title should be short yet specific, not general: a reader, attracted by a title, may be disappointed if he finds the paper is about only one specialized aspect of the subject promised. Have you experienced such a disappointment?

Many journals require a Headline or Running title as well as the Title. An ingenious paraphrase of the Title can supplement the latter. For example, the Latin name of a species might appear in the Title and the common name in the Running title.

If the journal prints key words, you can select them from your reservoir.

Summary

If the editor permits, compose the Summary in numbered paragraphs. The first should state – briefly – what you did. Then come the main results. Lists of values may be indigestible for your readers; so use words, supplemented by a few key values. State your conclusion in the last paragraph. If you have no succinct conclusion, you might write 'The effect of A upon B is discussed'.

If a summary is long, readers may look only at the first and last para-
(8) graphs. Although a well-written summary may be lifted by abstractors,

a long summary will be shortened, perhaps by the omission of what you consider vital parts.

Write the Summary in the past tense, except perhaps the last paragraph.

Some journals print the Summary in small type. How odd!

An abstract is not the same as a summary.

Introduction to a paper

The Introduction should state the problem, and perhaps ask a question. The objective must be clear. If you modified your objective after you began the work, give the current version. Do you still think you asked the right question?

The quoting of numerous papers in the Introduction is no longer good practice. [If much has been published, and you think it warrants a review, write that separately and submit it to an editor.] Refer to papers that, taken together, show that a problem exists. If another paper gives many references, refer to that. However, beware of lifting references – from that paper – together with misquotations of information from the original papers. That has been done.... For example, one abstractor supposed that *Kaninchen* meant little dog; and Yamane's work on the rabbit [*Kaninchen* means rabbit] has gone into the literature as being on the dog. For this and other cautionary tales, see Hartree (1976). For the extraordinary tale of O. Uplavici, an author who never lived, see Roland (1976).

In the last sentence of the Introduction, it is accepted practice to state the conclusion. A reader can better appreciate the evidence that follows if he knows what conclusion it is supporting. However, this version of the conclusion must be brief. Some authors repeat much of the Summary in the Introduction. That is not an acceptable practice.

Materials and Methods

If the description of materials is short it may be included in Methods. Avoid trade names if practicable, not to avoid advertising, but because they may not be understood abroad. [Do you know what Klampits or Barbistors are? or what Skellysolve means?] If you use a local name for polymethyl methacrylate or other compound, give the chemical name at first mention of the trade name.

Write what you did in operational order. Invert 'The urn was dated after restructuring' to 'The urn was reconstructed, then dated'. You should so describe the methods you used that others can repeat the

experiments. You must be concise, yet you must not omit essential
(9) detail. If you used 'alcohol' say which alcohol. If you controlled, or
even measured, the humidity and ventilation in an animal room, say so:
they may be nearly as important as temperature. If you centrifuged a
suspension, say whether supernatant or pellet was used for the next
operation. Similarly, if you filtered a suspension, say which part was
retained; it has not always been easy for a reader to conjecture. On the
other hand, there is no more need to tell us that the results were
analysed by computer (unless you state which program was used) than
there is to state that weighings were done on a balance, unless novel
methods were used.

If you used controls, permit no doubt about their nature. The reader
may not be able to guess what you omitted for each control.

If your paper is about a new method, ask a visitor or a technician to
test your description by applying the method in your absence. The result
of the omission of one detail can be illuminating.

Results

Before you write about your Results it may be advisable to study Units
and quantities (p. 23) and Tables (p. 22).

Replicate observations should not usually be given. Instead, offer the
mean and a measure of the variability if you can. The range is not
satisfactory; if there are enough replicates for the range to be of use then
there are enough for estimating the standard deviation (S.D.) of one
observation, the standard error of the mean (S.E.M.) or the coefficient of
variation (C.V.). Give the number of observations or the degrees of
(10) freedom within parentheses: 12.65 ± 0.22 (12). Perhaps you can make a
pooled estimate of the variance (or other statistic) from the whole study.
You can then give individual uncluttered values.

Journals ask for tables and figures to be clear without reference to the
text. This requires concise explanation in legends, an explanation of
abbreviations, and care in the avoidance of repetition in the text and in
other legends.

Discussion and Conclusion

The Discussion must not be so long as to deter a reader, yet it must
contain logical argument. Do not repeat descriptions of other people's
findings if they are in the Introduction; refer to that. Avoid summarizing
your results in the Discussion. Mention them, take them as read or refer
to a table or even to the Summary (quote the paragraph number).
Enlarge upon the significance of your new results and explain how they

add to existing knowledge. You may have formulated your problem as a question in the Introduction. If you can now give the answer, that facilitates discussion.

(11)   Think critically, not only about other people's work but about your own. For example, ask yourself 'Can my hypothesis be refuted? Can my results have another explanation?' Maier (1933) told the students in one of two large groups that, were they unable to solve the problem given to them, they should try to ignore their first approach and seek an altogether different line. (The other group, the control, was not told.) This worked; yet it is difficult to achieve such 'lateral thinking', as de Bono (1967) calls the modern development. The following example shows how important is such 'no-prejudice rethinking'. Two authors published graphs to prove their thesis that xanthine oxidase and the Schardinger enzyme (aldehyde oxidase) are distinct enzymes. Later, their graphs were used by another author to confirm the opposite (now accepted) view that the enzymes are identical. Had those first authors given their results more thought, they too might have reversed their conclusion. The literature contains abundant examples of inconclusive thinking. Writers should take care not to add to them by publishing in haste.

W. Pauli wrote 'I don't mind your thinking slowly: I mind your publishing faster than you can think.' [Translated by Mackay (1977).]

(12)   *Conclusion.* If you are fortunate, your Message (or part of it) may survive in text-books – although you may not be given a whole sentence! So the Conclusion needs precise wording. Your conclusion may appear (legitimately) three times: in the Discussion, the Summary and the Introduction. Do not repeat the wording; paraphrase it. If the reader has not understood one version, another may help him. Use the shortest version for the Summary.

Parting remarks. Perhaps you have not yet reached a conclusion, but have contributed towards one. You may like to end with 'Parting remarks'. Make them short, but do not bring 'final' into the heading.

References, Bibliography or Literature cited

Write each reference on a card. Arrange the cards in order and give them to the typist at the final typing of your paper. This scheme leads to fewer errors than does retyping the references at every retyping of the paper. Each journal arranges references in a particular style, which should be followed. Give the typist a copy of the journal to provide an example of style. If references in the text are made by superior digits, avoid 'the value was 24^2'; change to 'the value was 24 (ref. 2)'.

(13) Check the typed list against the original papers. Also check that the spelling of names in text and Bibliography agree. Inconsistencies and errors are *very* common in papers submitted to editors. (See Numbering, p. 23.)

Written English

Written English is nearly the same as spoken English – at their best. Grandiloquence has no place in scientific writing. We need to convey ideas effectively, to make it easy for the reader to understand what we write, not to exhibit our vocabulary. Indeed, those who use pompous language may even be suspected of having nothing important to say! Try to envisage the reader; write especially for him, in a manner not too technical, not too elementary. Write as though you are talking to a reader, telling him about your experiments, but restrain colloquialisms.

(14) *Clear English.* Ask yourself often: would M'Fline [p. x (1)] understand what I write? Write short sentences, but not all of them so short as to produce a staccato effect, as on p. 43 (73). Cure a staccato passage by linking two sentences (as I have done here with a 'but'), but do this only seldom, so as to keep to 'one idea per sentence' with occasional exceptions. A satisfying sentence has two main verbs (Perttunen, 1975).

(15) If you train yourself to speak well, that will help you to develop a good written style. In conversation, choose words with care, enunciate deliberately, speak grammatically.

Mutual editing

(16) In courses on rapid reading, one is told not to go back to re-read a passage. A trained reader may not let himself return to a difficult sentence whose meaning was not grasped. How can you discover such passages in your own writing? One way is to put the paper away for a month [p. 2 (5)]. This may be impractical. Another is to have a colleague read your paper. Ask him both to make general comments and to mark every sentence he had to read twice. If he is critical, thank him nevertheless, for, if he fails to understand you, others might fail too and your Message will be lost.

For nearly 2000 years it has been known that we see other people's faults more easily than our own. (Parable of the mote and beam, Matthew 7, iii.) Moreover, it is fun to cross out words in other people's papers. Therefore, make a deal with a colleague; if he will let you 'correct' his papers, you will let him correct yours. Do not use red ink, which is umbragenic; green is more soothing.

You may have noted a repetition above. That is deliberate, because emphasis is needed. Hundreds of the errors I have seen, in papers that had already been accepted but not yet edited, ought to have been seen by a critical colleague and then corrected – before submission.

However senior you be, ignore the 'statuskline', or hierarchy, and ask for constructive criticism, not flattery, from your juniors. Such editing should be good training for them.

Literary style

(17) *Noun adjectives.* In English, nouns may be used as adjectives, that is, as modifiers of a true noun. One might write 'an oil engine needs engine oil' or 'glass bottles are made of bottle glass'. But such use may lead to confusion unless undertaken with care. For such terms as 'dog meat' or 'cat fish' make it clear which of the two meanings is intended. 'Rapid gas apparatus deterioration' is better written as 'Rapid deterioration of gas apparatus' and 'product treatment' as 'treatment of the product'. If you dislike recurrent 'of', the occasional genitive case may be used. [P. 32 (70).]

It is not suggested that nouns should never be used adjectivally. Many are so used satisfactorily, including hydrogen bond, gold size, oak tree, steel plate, SI units.

When two or more nouns are used as adjectives of one noun, the phrase may become inelegant. Consider the following: isotope dilution assay results; pH 4.4 buffer; multiple conductor galvanized angle steel pylon system; scanning electron beam annealing apparatus control; we devised a new short chain fluorocarbon aerosol can valve. Such phrases are difficult to comprehend; the reader finds that each successive noun is not the real noun; he has mentally to store the words until he reaches the substantive being modified. Therefore, avoid long adjectival phrases, or stacked modifiers as Woodford (1970) calls them. Even if the modifier contains no noun adjective, it may be troublesome, as this example shows: a frequently heated and therefore deeply coloured viscous solution.... The use of hyphens may lead to improvement of some phrases, but rewriting usually gives the best solution.

(18) Note that '*in vivo*', 'excess' and '*de novo*' are not adjectives, but that 'subliminal', 'optimal', 'minimal', 'maximal' are. Write 'test *in vitro*' not *in vitro* test. People would not write 'in glass test'.

Comparatives. A passage that contains a comparative sometimes causes
(19) difficulty: what does 'lions eat more than antelopes' mean? Make clear what is more than what, and only compare things that are comparable. Instead of 'starch yielded more glucose than maltose' write either

'...than did maltose' or 'starch produced a greater yield of glucose than of maltose'. Do not omit 'those in' from 'bearings in steam engines lasted longer than diesel engines'. 'Lymphocytes from treated patients were less sensitive than were untreated patients' needs 'those from' after 'were'.

Wrongly attached participle. Every verb needs a subject, an operator, either actual or understood. One of the most common errors submitted for publication is exemplified by 'having completed the observations the telescope...' or 'a bend was observed in the bridge using a strain gauge'. Was the bridge really using a gauge? Phrases such as the following make people laugh. After standing in boiling water for 2 h, examine the flask; electronic devices should be made safe before leaving the laboratory; and goggles are required to do the experiment. Yet such (20) errors (aberrations, faults, lapses...) are often submitted to editors. Read what Fowler [B (8)] or the authors of style books listed in Chapter (21) Seven have written on Unattached, Wrongly attached or Dangling participles and infinitives.

Gerund. A participle may become a kind of noun (called a gerund), as in 'Writing a paper'. If the adding of 'the' and 'of' (as before and after 'adding' near the beginning of this sentence) makes grammatical sense, the -ing word is a gerund. Applying this test, you can see that 'Using a dynamometer, the tractive effort was measured' is not allowable because 'Using' is a wrongly attached verb here, not a gerund. [On the other hand, in 'Applying this test, you...' the 'you' was the subject, and the phrase is allowable.] Change the sentence to 'Using..., we measured...' or to 'A dynamometer was used for the measuring of the tractive...' or add 'By' → 'By using a...'.

Be ever alert for dangling verbs. So many sentences start with 'Judging by' or 'Based on' that these participles are becoming accepted for use in (22) that way. Even so, let other words that end in -ing or -ed warn you to ensure that each is either a gerund or is properly attached to an operator. 'Using' is not a preposition, so whenever you write the word, tell us *who* was using or make sure the word is a gerund.

(23) *Pudder, or needless words.* If you put aside your draft, then examine it (24) later, this is the time to expunge what Houp & Pearsall [B (4)] call 'empty words'. Such phrases as 'It is worth pointing out in this context that' may be deleted without affecting the meaning. So may the following.

It is significant to note the fact that   relevant to mention here that
The results reported here demonstrate that   It is known that
It should be borne in mind in this connection that   found to be
Such phrases, which correspond to spoken anderms, are not needed in
scientific reports. Many phrases may be shortened. For 'It is plainly
(25) demonstrable from the curves presented in Fig. 2' write 'Fig. 2 shows'.
If a piece is introduced by 'Needless to say', why say it? 'Recent' is
usually superfluous if the date is given in the references. Usually 'we
(26) wish to thank' means 'we thank', 'has been shown to be' means 'is',
and 'proved to be' means 'were'. 'It can be seen in Table 4 that' may
be omitted and '(Table 4)' placed after the statement. 'Concerning' may
be replaced by 'on'; 'therefore' and 'consequently' may be cut to 'so'.
Indeed, 'so' is a neglected word.

The following phrases should each be cut to one word:

actual fact	absolute minimum	in an exhausted condition
all of	as to whether	join together
both of	by means of	knots per hour
foot pedal	completely full	large in size
given data	definitely proved	period of time
half of	exactly true	red in colour
in order to	falling down	round in shape
quite unique	first of all	weather conditions
very similar	flat plateau	would appear

As Strunk (1959) writes, 'Make every word count'.

(27) *Pronouns.* When you write 'it', 'this', 'which' or 'they', are you sure
the meaning is plain? Readers may be unwilling to search back for the
meaning of 'it'. A pronoun deputizes (usually) for the nearest previous
noun of the same number (singular or plural). If you have used a pronoun for a more distant noun, perhaps the noun should be repeated, as
'summary' is on p. 3 (8). We may know what the author means by
'seeds were placed in petri dishes which were then softened in water'.
However, if 'which' were to refer to something even more distant than
'seeds', we might not know.

A sentence that starts with 'It' should be examined critically. It may
be that the sentence starts, as this one does, with an 'It' that does not
refer to a previous noun, yet the reader momentarily expects it to do
that. So, turn 'It is believed that carbon dating gives...' to 'Carbon
dating is believed to give...'. Two other arguments against the starting
of a sentence with 'It' (needless words and distant reference) have been
explained above [(24), (27)].

Personal pronoun. An occasional 'I' need not be shunned. Indeed, 'I' may be desirable to dispel doubt about who did something. If you quote published results and then give yours, claim the latter. 'The author' might seem to mean the other writer, not you. If an 'I' seems out of place, the change from his work to yours may be indicated by the words 'in the present work', but elaborate avoidance of 'I' may be clumsy. [See (28) below.] Never, of course, write 'we' for yourself, or use 'I' immodestly or too often.

Personal pronouns should not appear in a summary because they will make an abstractor's task difficult.

Double hedging. Avoid repetition of the type 'may be...probable', 'seems that...could be possible' and 'it is supposed it might...in some cases'. Such hedging weakens discussion. If a writer is so unsure that he has to hedge, is he really ready to publish? One possibility seems to be that triple hedging may produce flabby writing, as it has done in this sentence.

Tense, mood and voice

An author usually writes about his new work in the simple past tense: 'I saw sparks' or 'sparks were seen'. Do not describe your results in the compound past tense; write 'were' not 'have been'. Other people's work is variously reported. Many authors use the present tense; some use the compound past tense, as in 'Nob has studied fossils'. A change in tense (28) helps us to distinguish between your work and his. Day [B (6)] explains why the present tense is desirable in the reporting of published work.

Working directions for a method are sometimes written in the imperative mood. This is done partly because it makes the most direct style.

The passive voice, commonly used to describe results, sometimes makes clumsy construction. Turn a passive phrase to direct style when you can. For example, turn 'oxygen is needed for combustion' to 'combustion needs oxygen. 'It is reported by Job' is better written as Job reports. 'Excavation was involved in the project' should be 'the project included excavation'. Sometimes a passive phrase may be avoided by writing 'I'.

Never 'subject a patient to examination' – examine him.

Choice of words

Beware of using words whose true meaning is not what you wish to convey. Here are some words that deserve especial care.

    case. I recommend you to read what Fowler, Partridge, Day or other

(29)   authority has written about 'case' (Chapter Seven). A sloppy misuse is
to make the word act as a pronoun – as in 'the above cases' – so that
the reader has to go back to find what the cases were. I have met cases
(many, many of them) where I could not be sure to what the writer
referred; did 'two cases' mean two experiments, two animals or two
observations on one animal? Replace 'case', if you can, by a word that
gives information, for example 'this mineral' or 'Expt 8'. Or shorten the
phrase, as in these examples: in most c. (usually, mostly); in this c.
(here); in all c. (always); in no c. (never); in that c. (so); in the c. of
(for, in); was the c. (was so, was true); the c. in question (this patient).
'In some c. this was the c.' needs no comment.

different is used too often. If two methods were used, 'different' is not
needed; if the methods were not different there would not be two. In
'...applied different torsions' replace different by various.

(30)   **due to** and **owing to**. 'Due to' is often written where 'owing to' would
be better. 'Due to' has the sense of caused by; 'owing to' has the sense
of because of. We may write 'the colour of the diamond was due to
impurities' but 'owing to impurities the diamond was coloured'. If 'Due
to' starts a sentence, that is probably wrong. Consider the sentence:
'Cardiac disease due to the use of drugs is not always fatal'. This
implies that the disease is caused by the drugs. If 'due to' be replaced
by owing to, we have the opposite meaning: the disease is not always
fatal, because drugs are used. Commas after disease and drugs make
the meaning clear: 'Cardiac disease, owing to the use of drugs, is not
always fatal'. Must we lose 'owing to' owing to incorrect substitution
by due to?

efficient describes processes whose efficiency can be measured. A writer
may mean effective. You may have devised a shaking machine, a cutter
or a warning device. Can you determine that it is efficient? A potentio-
meter-type power pack (for supplying desired voltages) was described
as 'efficient'. Engineers who read that such apparatus is efficient, which
it cannot be, may doubt the truth of other statements in the paper.

fact. When you write 'fact', do you truly mean undisputed knowledge?
Effect, hypothesis, observation, value, result, phenomenon or finding
may be more modest. 'These facts' may even be changed to words that
give information, for example 'these similarities'. 'Due to the fact that'
is better written as 'Because'. 'In spite of the fact that my results were
negative' is bettered on several counts by 'Despite my finding no effect'.
Strunk (1959) says 'the fact that' should be revised out of every sentence
in which it occurs. Careful writers do not describe their findings as facts.
A 'fact' reported by an author may be contraindicated by results from
another. This often happens.

minimal means lowest, smallest, and should not be written for small.

parameter is sometimes used unwisely. Variable might be safer.

varying means changing. The word is often used wrongly in place of variable, varied or various. [P. 26 (54).] Computations made with varying formulas would have only little value, whereas those made with various formulas might confirm one another.

which and **that**. If you are unsure about these words, recall the rule 'which describes, that defines'. Consider the phrases:

brown hens, which lay brown eggs, have yellow...
brown hens that lay brown eggs have yellow...

The first implies that brown hens lay brown eggs and also have the yellow character. The second means that those particular brown hens that lay brown eggs have it. Confirm your decision through the commas; if they are needed, write 'which'. Another example follows.

A pronoun that cannot easily be identified with a noun is said to dangle. Dangling pronouns (DP), which may be 'it', 'ones', 'they' and 'these', are troublesome.

The first sentence *defines* the DP, and there are no commas. The second sentence *describes* the DP as troublesome. Note the two commas, one before 'which', one before 'are'; if the parenthetic remark between them be omitted the sentence still makes sense – 'Dangling pronouns are troublesome'.

Plain words. In general, use short rather than long words if they have the same meaning. Often this means use words from Anglo-Saxon rather than from Latin. (See Words, p. 39.) Write:

have, not possess; enough, not sufficient;
about, not approximately, of the order of or *circa*;
use, not utilize or employ (employ implies payment; did you pay?)

'Show' may be better than demonstrate, disclose, exhibit or reveal. However, do not eschew a long word or a word derived from Latin if it conveys the meaning better than another: 'syrup' is an aqueous solution that cannot be called watery; 'expunge' is more vigorous than 'remove' [p. 9 (24)]; 'reveal' is apt on p. 23 (48).

When you write the first words in the following list do you mean the second, or vice versa? Accordance (accord); brackets (parentheses); generally (usually); wire (cable); if (when, whether); plug (socket).

Mathematical terms are often used for non-mathematical meanings, which is undesirable if an ordinary word exists. For example, it is not advisable to write 'centre' (a mathematical point) if you mean middle, or 'degree' if you mean extent. For graphs, write 'filled' symbol, not solid; and 'unbroken', not solid, line. 'All' is usually better than 100%.

In mathematics, an area has only two dimensions, so use another word when you refer to more than a surface. In scientific writing, 'negative' is best reserved for 'minus' and for electric polarity; there are plenty of other words for none. 'No response' is more scientific than 'response was negative'.

Avoid the unscientific use of $\pm$ for 'about' or for with and without (when $+$ or 0 is meant), and do not use equals ($=$) for 'means' or indicates. Eight plus and $8+$ are not so scientific as >8.

Elegant variation. English abounds in near synonyms – different words that have almost the same meaning. Examples include begin, commence, start, launch, originate, initiate, auspicate. Repetition of a word within a sentence is considered to be bad style, which may be avoidable with synonyms. However, in scientific writing, a synonym should be used only if its meaning is clear. Repeat a word if the sense so requires. There may be a case for a synonym where a technical word might not be understood by all, but the writer must make it clear that the two words mean the same thing. At first use, some authors write both words. [See The solidus, p. 20 (43).] Repetition may sometimes be avoided by the rewriting of a sentence. If a sentence has many 'and's, try replacing one of them by 'then'.

Homonyms. Many English words have more than one meaning. Where possible, use a word that has only one meaning. Never, in one passage, use the same word for different meanings, as for example in 'Factor V varied by a factor of 4' or 'For preservation one can can it'.

'Normal' has often been used as a trouble saver and has so many meanings that it should be avoided where possible. Normal temperature may mean 0 or 37.4 °C. 'Normal saline' is less descriptive than 'physiological saline'. Normal should no longer be used to describe solutions. The accepted form is mol l^{-1}. Because mol l^{-1} is clumsy, is not an adjective and is unsuitable for speech, many people prefer M, and a few prefer mol/l.

The use of existing words for new meanings causes confusion, especially to M'Fline. Chapter Five gives examples; here are others.

'Cell' is overworked; 'cuvette' is better in spectrophotometry. 'Reduce' has various meanings. Avoid the word or clarify it as appropriate.

'Figure' is used for picture, pattern, diagram, shape, number, digit or numeral, quantity or amount, price and value, as well as for calculate and even for think. The reservation of 'figure' for the first meaning seems desirable. A number, such as 247, is composed of digits or numerals; 24.7 mg is a quantity; 2.47 in a table is a value. The abbreviation for

(31)   ordinal 'Number' is 'no.'. Cardinal 'number', used for quantities, should not be written 'no.'. Write '...number of turns in coil no. 6...'.

(32)   *Foreign words.* If you use foreign words when English words will convey the meaning, you risk being accused of affectation. You also risk our failing to understand you. Sometimes the spelling or grammar is faulty. 'Media' is plural, as are phenomena and capita. Hence 'per capita' means per heads. Did you realize that?

Conveyance of ideas without element of doubt or exaggeration

You may think this fuss over precision in the use of words 'is only cosmetic'. But, if you prefer not to take rules of grammar and usage seriously, may I plead as follows?

First, convey your Message clearly. Dixon [B (12)] writes in a breezy style, yet his meaning is plain.

Secondly, do not be conservative about names. We have discarded vitriol, jar, fuming spirits of muriatic acid, candle power, probable error. So let us drop a.m. and p.m., formalin, glycerine, h.p., pet. ether, soda, centigrade. Is it fair to expect young people to learn archaic names as well as systematic terms?

(33)   Thirdly, please add no nails to the coffins of useful words. We have almost lost 'very', formerly a very useful word. Consider that last phrase: did the second 'very' affect the meaning? The demise is hastened by such thoughtless uses as 'very unique' and 'very level'; yet on occasion we need the word. [P. 7 (13).] 'Surely', 'doubtless' and their synonyms no longer mean without doubt; 'no doubt' they will go.

Various words that should have the sense of 'ultimate' are losing their meanings through misuse; they include most, extremely, fatal, infinitely, perfect, vital, absolutely. Watch them.

The meaning of 'quite' is reversing: 'his method is quite good' now means less good than 'good'. 'A certain amount' now usually means an imprecisely known, an *un*certain, amount. Other reversals include release, which formerly meant *allow* to go. Now it is used for publish, that is *push* out, as in 'Provisional data release'. Philip Norman (1980) uses the term paranym for such opposites. In politics the use of paranyms is common, but scientists should not use them.

'Fig. 5 clearly shows' is common. Had 'clearly' been omitted, a reader might believe the statement, but 'clearly' alerts him, and the element of persuasion makes him sceptical. 'Clearly' is becoming a paranym. 'Plainly visible in the figure' has the same effect.

I appeal to you to use words with care.

Cosmetics

He who spurns meticulous writing may write: 'Believing the shape to be important a diet was prepared on a square plate which the patient ate.' We know what the writer meant despite his three errors, but does that make such writing acceptable?

Good workmanship endures

After you are elected a Nobel laureate, people will look at your early papers. You will not want to squirm with embarrassment as they discover that you once thought 'accordance' meant accord or that '4 times more than' meant the same as 4 times as many as. [For argument, see p. 24 (52).] Scientists who look back at their early papers feel (justifiable) pleasure on finding good writing. I recommend you similarly to invest in the future.

Craftsmanship takes time to learn but is worth the effort. The object of a writer should be to convey information with minimal effort from the reader. Although grammatical customs, like etiquette, are not all logically defensible, if you ignore them you may obscure your meaning.

You may think 'There are so many rules and pitfalls! How can I remember them all?' At first you cannot. But, if you persist, you will find that clear writing is a craft in which to take pleasure.

Language in flux

English is changing. That is desirable to meet changing needs, but it is not desirable to lose meanings of useful words. When a new word is needed, it seems better to make one than to add to the plethora of homonyms by taking an existing word. An example of such invention is 'capacitor' to replace condenser, which has other meanings. We need (34) a word for s.e.m. – without the 'error' connotation. Another could be 'andor' to avoid the algebraic and/or. But let us shun such horrors as 'uniformization'.

Certain changed usages are common and may become established. Examples now occurring include: aliquot to mean *any* measured amount; a number were; these results suggest; ultraviolet light; under the circumstances; detergents and soap; restructured; significant not qualified by statistically; 100-volume H_2O_2; heighth; caustic, coronary, medical and other adjectives used as nouns. The first few examples may be acceptable. Others are not. No doubt you could add to the list, but do you find the trend agreeable?

Revision of the script must not be hurried

A writer's work is so familiar to him that he may be bored as he reads
what he has written. The intense concentration needed for revision
(35)   cannot be maintained for long. Therefore, I urge you to read only one
page of typescript at a time, and to

READ IT SLOWLY.

While you read, imagine that M'Fline is looking over your shoulder.
[P. x (1).] What you have written should make sense, not only as you
read it, but when you read it aloud. Make it sound like intelligent con-
(36)   versation. Where you pause, insert a stop. Ask a friend to read the script
to you. Where he stumbles, rewrite the passage.

Critical revision is more necessary than writers realize. Even some of
the books on writing that are listed in Chapter Seven contain lapses of
style and errors. So, BE VIGILANT. Let your aim be to make such people
as myself redundant. The species does not seem to be endangered!

Extend your vigilance to repetition as well as to style and sense. In
some papers, the Introduction and the Discussion contain similar
passages. In your script you may find parts of a method described in a
legend or in notes to a table as well as in Results. Avoid such repetition
if you can. If your Conclusion is repeated, as suggested elsewhere, paraphrase it. Other parts, the comprehension of which is paramount, may
be said again differently, introduced perhaps by 'in other words'. Use
this device sparingly, however, or you will be in trouble, and so shall I.
For an example see p. 2 (5) with p. 9 (23), or p. 1 (3) and (4).

A great deal of needless repetition and verbiage is to be found, now as
in the past, in so very many published papers, yet it may be that the
authors were completely unaware of their unnecessary repetitions,
a possibility that can be adduced as yet one more good reason that
authors should have for asking a colleague both to read and to comment on their scientific writings. You may like to write out the previous
sentence and, as you write, prune it to less than half. It can be done.
Please do not spoil it for others by marking the print.

Spelling

Some words have alternative spellings. For example, show, gray, tyre,
acknowledgement, disk, neutralize. If the choice is yours, use the spelling
that better represents the pronunciation. Some words are spelt differently
in the UK and the USA. A few publishers allow a writer to use either,
but he must be consistent.

Stops or punctuation ,;:.

The common stops may still be considered to comprise a hierarchy: new paragraph, full stop (period or full point), colon, semicolon, spaced dash, comma. A lesser stop cannot govern (control, or take precedence over) a greater. The spaced dash and the colon do not always fit into the hierarchy.

(37) *A new paragraph* (NP), in general, denotes a change of subject. In good prose, one notion leads to another, which makes this rule difficult to apply. Because short paragraphs can look irritating, long ones boring, skilful compromise may be needed. If you want each NP to show in your published paper, you MUST either indicate each one by indention or mark it on your script. [See p. viii.]

Colon. The phrase before a colon is general; the phrase (or phrases) after it is (are) particular. Therefore, no sentence should contain two colons. Traditionally a colon does not end a sentence, but a full stop does, so a colon should not occur after a phrase that refers to more than one sentence each having its own full stop. For example, if 'as follows' is followed by complete sentences, use a full stop, not a colon, after 'follows'. The following type of confusion is submitted to editors.

The solution contained: glucose: 2 g, NaCl: 3 g and urea: 4 g.

The piece is better written as follows.

The solution contained: glucose, 2 g; NaCl, 3 g; and urea, 4 g.

Similarly '...conditions (time: 25 min, current: 2A)' should have its comma replaced by a semicolon and its colons by commas.

  Some people would banish the colon; yet it can have a real use. Please help it to survive and to keep its value – greater than that of the comma, less than that of a full stop.

Semicolons separate two or more related clauses. Many examples appear in this book. For an example that shows the distinction between colon and semicolon, see p. 19 (39).

The comma signals a short pause. Use commas cannily, and perhaps more often than some writers use them, to prevent over-reading – as in the example that follows. Where two adjacent nouns belong in different clauses separation should be achieved with a comma – for example after clauses.

  Children used to be taught not to put a comma before 'and'. The logic is as follows. We may mean '*a* and *b* and *c*', but we write *a, b* and *c.* One 'and' is replaced by a comma, but no comma is needed before the retained 'and'. In the phrases 'chalk and clay' and 'tides were measured and recorded' no comma is needed. The 'and' is the joining variety and could be represented by &. There is another kind of 'and': 'the cats were fed on meat and worms were given to the fish'. Your probable hesitation could have been avoided if a comma had appeared after 'meat'. Here is another example: '...is dissolved in 5 mol l^{-1} NaOH and 2 mol l^{-1} KOH is added'. And another: 'The chairman was head of the physics lab and the principal of the maths lab was elected vice-chairman'. So, when two phrases are linked by 'and', a comma is needed to show that they *are* two phrases. Curiously, the superstition does not ban the comma before 'or', or before 'but'.

A comma is needed before an 'and' that separates negative and positive notions, as in 'Do not write too much between full stops and present the information in small packets for easy understanding' and in 'The alloy is made by adding Sn to Pb and Zn is rigorously excluded'.

A comma can change a meaning. 'The sky is not black, as Zob proved' means Zob proved the sky is not black. Without the comma the phrase means Zob proved the sky is black.

Commas may be used in pairs, *as here*, to enclose a parenthetical remark. The latter is treated on p. 20 (42).

(38) *Dashes.* The four symbols, hyphen (-), en rule (–), minus (−) and em rule (—), are represented on the typewriter by one sign popularly called a dash. The meanings of the *hyphen* and the *em rule* (or long dash) are
(39) opposite: the hyphen joins words or pieces of a word; the em rule pushes words apart with a pause rather longer than that signalled by a comma. Because each sign is useful and has its own meaning it seems desirable to preserve their identities. [Glossary, p. xi.]
(40) The en rule (short dash) has various uses including that in 1968–84. Spaces are not needed. Write 'from 2 to 28' not from 2–28. Solutions are sometimes described thus:

hydrochloric acid–sodium chloride
ethanol–methanoic acid–water

Avoid the confusion by writing 'a mixture of hydrochloric acid and sodium chloride' or 'mixture of ethanol, methanoic acid and water (3:1:10)'.

The hyphen has many uses. Because the rules cannot be condensed to a few lines I shall do no more than offer suggestions and examples.

A hyphen joins words to make adjectives: if a hypothesis is well known it is a well-known hypothesis; an example is the all-or-none hypothesis. Do not join adverbs that end in -ly. Write 'vitamin-deficient and little-used diet' but 'a rarely eaten food'; also write 'X-ray-induced and chemically induced mutations'. A hyphen can change a meaning: a large impulse counter is not the same as a large-impulse counter; 5 day sessions differ from 5-day sessions; were the hyphen to be omitted from 'little-used' above the meaning would change.

(41)   Hyphens may be used to join nouns to make an adjective (vanadium-steel pin, noun-adjective phrase), but if this be done with multiple nouns the result is unsatisfactory, as in negative-particle-analyser procedure and Lipidon-48H-column chromatography. Such phrases should be turned about: e.g. ablacillin-C-induced effect should be effect induced by ablacillin C.

Consult a recently issued and well-produced catalogue for help with hyphens in chemical names. Catalogues from Koch–Light and BDH [B (20)] have been useful.

Link a prefix (non-, post-, etc.) to a noun by a hyphen. M'Fline [p. x (1)] is then warned to look in the dictionary for the noun instead of searching under n or p. Postparturition might confuse him. Separation by a hyphen may aid the pronunciation of words such as sub-unit, co-operate and co-worker.

If you invent a new name, for example Q effect or HK mesons, do not use hyphens. Copper compound should not be joined by a hyphen; nor should t test.

(42)   *Parentheses* is the name for round brackets ( ). Parenthesis also means an aside or explanation between two commas, dashes or parentheses (as here) within a sentence. If such a parenthetic remark is left out, the sentence should still make sense and be grammatically complete. If the remark is a complete sentence give it a capital letter and its own full stop, surround the whole with parentheses or square brackets, and place it after, not within, its parent sentence. [P. 28 (60).] Although '(Table 2)' may appear within a sentence, it is better for a longer phrase such as '(See for example Table 2.)' to be treated as a sentence. If the parenthesis is only part of a sentence, the full stop goes outside.

(43)   *The solidus* (diagonal) is used to mean 'per' as in wires/cable. Confusion may arise if the diagonal is used for other meanings, such as dates or contractions. Do not write 'g/l of KCl': the solution is not per litre of KCl but of KCl per litre. Equally unscientific, though common, is the note that 2 mg/kg of a drug were given. Write '2 mg of drug per kg...' or '...drug (2 mg/kg) was given'. The argument also applies to '...p.p.m. CO_2'. A solidus may make 'response/dose' better than dose–response.

The solidus brings a mathematical formula into a line, thus: $(a+b^2)/3p$. Fractions extending through two lines are ugly and expensive.

Initial letters. Avoid starting a sentence with a lower-case abbreviation, such as p- or α-, or with van der, if you can. A sentence should not start with a numeral. [P. 24 (52).] If you find such a sentence, either rewrite it or spell out the number. This practice is especially important when the previous sentence ends with a numeral, symbol or abbreviation: change '...found in 1984. 73 μg of iodine was...' to '...found in 1984. Iodine 73 μg, was...'.

Abbrevns & cntrctns

The smallest symbol in the printer's fount, the dot (.), has many meanings. The second best-known function of the dot is that of indi-
(44) cating abbreviations. The abbreviative presence – or the absence – of the dot evokes more editorial adrenaline than does that of any of the larger
(45) symbols. So here I indicate practices but do not dare to instruct.

Some publishers omit the dot from Expt, Mr and Dr as well as from other contractions that include the first and last letters of the word. Some words (Miss, log, bus) have been with us so long that few people give them a stop. Units (g, mm, F, min, h) take no full stop (period) and plurals no 's'.

A few abbreviations are ugly. 'Viz.' saves only two characters from 'namely', and '*ca.*' from about. Approx., too, is bettered by about. Cf., which means compare not 'see', may usually be deleted. The *Biochemical Journal*, in its instructions to authors [B (2)], gives a list of abbreviations useful to all scientists.

Abbreviations, of long terms or names of materials to which you often refer, are best collected into a footnote on the first page. The names should be given in full in the Summary.

Headings or captions

As a novelist uses dialogue to make a page look interesting, so a scientific writer uses headings and subheads. They help to make a paper readable, and guide the inquirer to parts he wants to read again. Use many. Write subheads for the Discussion; they can be truly helpful.

A heading should contain a noun. A lone adjective should not be used; add 'part' to Experimental.

Make your headings work. Be cunning. Perhaps you have used the 'in-
(46) other-words' device in the text but still desire emphasis. Try to include,

in a heading, the notion that needs emphasis, but use different expressions in heading and text. [See p. 17 (35) on revision, or p. 30 (65).] Repetition of a heading in the text is undesirable. A heading may ask a question [p. 23 (49)]. The Introduction to a normal paper should not need that word as heading, which is as superfluous as is 'Notice' on an obvious notice. However, if you can put information into a heading for the Introduction, that could be useful. For example, can you describe your problem in words different from those in the Title?

Tables

A table needs a title, probably supplemented by an explanation. The heading to each column should include units, so that each entry is a number. If your quantities are large or small, use the prefixes M, m, p, etc. Avoid using $\times 10^{-3}$ in a heading because a reader may wonder – have you divided by 10^3 or must he do so?

Study the tables in the journal of your choice; then conform with the style so that the editor does not have to make rearrangements.

(47)   Indigestible tables with many or cumbersome values deter readers. Trim the values even if you risk losing an occasional significant digit. Methods exist for calculating significant digits. One digit more than is meaningful does no good whatever. The S.E.M. should have no more digits after the decimal than does the mean. Should the argument require results from several experiments, and they cannot be condensed or pooled [see p. 5 (10)], consider dividing them into two or more tables.

Measures of variation MUST be defined without possibility of misunderstanding. Unfortunately S.D. and S.E. (see p. 10) have often been used interchangeably. In one paper submitted, the standard error of the mean was so described several times, but the formula, given three times (in text, table and note), was that for S.D. Never forget that your calculated measure of variation only *estimates* that of the population of which your results are a sample. When *n* is small, the S.D. has little if any meaning.

Illustrations

When an experiment provides many observations they may be better presented in a graph than as a table. The same information is not usually allowed to appear in both forms. For many people a diagram is easier to grasp and to remember than is a table.

The horizontal co-ordinate of a graph represents what we select (time, weight, frequency...) and the vertical co-ordinate what we measure. If the origin of either axis is not zero, indicate this by a break in the line.

A graph needs an indication of precision, such as an estimate of confidence limits, or symbols of a size to indicate the s.e.m.

Think about response/dose curves and related subjects in logarithmic terms. If one adds 1, 2, 3, 4, 5, 6 units of reagent, the jump from 1 to 2 is 1 unit but the concentration is increased × 2. The jump from 5 to 6 is also 1 unit but the relative increase is only × 1.2. For some studies it is better to arrange that each rise is proportionally the same. If your graph is then crowded at one end, try a non-linear scale. Convert doses into log doses or use log graph paper; or try reciprocals, squares or square roots; try dissimilar conversions for the two co-ordinates. Such (48) conversion may use the graphic area more effectively, and it may reveal a straight line.

(49) **Are all your numbers correct?**

If 'dependent' is misspelt the sub-editor can correct that. If 265 appears for 205 a context may not help. Editors' time is wasted over incorrect numbers actually detected, but the true total of errors is unknown. In a table it is unlikely that anybody but the author can check the values.

Numbering of figures, tables and references during their preparation

If you number the tables and figures from first writing you may have to (50) change the numbers as your paper develops. Instead of numbers, use letters that describe tables and figures to you privately. Before the final typing, change to numbers. With this scheme you are unlikely to leave a wrong number in the text.

Literature cited poses an analogous problem. At first I use the Harvard System – names and year in the text. If the journal requires numbers, I 'correct' the script at a later stage.

Units and quantities

Use SI units. Some old units (e.g. bar, calorie, mm Hg) may survive for a time, but when old units are used, SI units should be given too.

What is still sometimes called molecular weight is a ratio rather than a weight. At present this ratio is printed M_r. The inferior $_r$ is typographically unsatisfactory, which may be one reason for the unpopularity of M_r. Dixon (1983) explains why relative molecular mass is a better term than molecular weight.

Make your units unambiguous. If you 'add 2 mol l^{-1} HCl', either say

how much you added or that you 'made the solution 2 mol l⁻¹ with
respect to HCl'.

Times should be given on the 24-h system, e.g. 08h 30. Dates are
printed without stops (06 April 1985) or with hyphens (06-iv-1985). To
sandwich the day between bigger units (April 6, 1985) is illogical.
Logically we should proceed from large to small units (year, month,
day, hour, min..., thus 1985-04-06...) as astronomers do and as other
people do with weights and measures. This logical system is described
in British Standard 4795 [B (19)] and in ISO-2014; 1975. The system
may take a long time to be accepted everywhere.

(51)
When you offer a series of values, do not repeat the units. Write '3
and 4 g' not 3 g and 4 g. Another kind of repetition should also be
avoided. From 'the percentage was 8 %' omit % or write 'the proportion
was 8 %'. Write 'the pH was 8', and 'the voltage was 8' or state that
the PD was 8 V. People do not write that the ohmage was 8 ohms or
that the hourage was 08h 00, because the unitage should not be repeated.

Modern units go up and down in steps of 1000. Avoid other steps if
you can. The Ångström is redundant – and mispronounced! Concentrations other than mol l⁻¹ are expressed as parts per thousand or per
million (p.p.m.). Concentrations should no longer be expressed as %.

Units named after people are spelt without a capital, but symbols for
such units do have capitals: thus, watt and W, joule and J, pascal and
Pa, dalton and D.

Because l, 1 and I may be confused, especially in scripts, L sometimes
replaces l for litre.

Doubtful quantities. The sign % indicates a ratio, a pure fraction without
units. A writer who describes a concentration in % then writes 'it rose
2 %' leaves you to guess whether he means 2 percentage units or × 1.02.
If you have no interest in decoding, the information is lost. Percentages
are best reserved for comparisons. But they must be clear. Replace
'150 % more than' by 2½ times.

(52)
'3 times more than' means '4 times as much as'. If this surprises you,
extrapolate down to once more than, which obviously means twice as
much as. A dilution of 1:5 means 1 in 6. Here, too, the logic can be
appreciated by consideration of 1:1. Because of confusion, it is best not
to write 'times more than' or diluted 1:10. What does '4 times less than'
mean? One time more than means twice as much as, so once less than
must mean none. Hence 4 times less than means minus 3 times. Such
terms should not be used. Other expressions to be avoided include
'250 % lower than' and 'divided by a third'. A reader took time to
realize that 2.1/2 was not 1.05 but 2½.

'A plate 90 × 100 mm' is not scientific. Write '...90 mm × 100 mm'.

Paradox. A scientist makes observations to perhaps three or four digits, and processes the results on an eight-digit calculator. A good writer then discards meaningless digits and uses words with care. But some writers use words [see above and p. 31 (68)] with a precision of only one significant digit!

Apparatus, materials and writing techniques

To write well one must be in a suitable state of mind. Such a 'mood' cannot be commanded. Seating, desk, pen and paper can help. The chair should be of the right height and should have a back-rest at kidney height, but nowhere else. This will allow one to sit upright in comfort. Good posture is important for another reason: a crouching posture may lead to back-ache in later life. For the good of your health, I strongly recommend that you alternate between sitting and standing. Such a scheme is not difficult to arrange.

Because you may rewrite many times, a pen that glides easily is more than desirable. Choose paper that suits you, and write only on the smoother top surface – the side from which the watermark reads the right way. Leave wide margins, and do not write much on a sheet; the pages need not be filled. Generous use of paper and standard left margin of 40 mm facilitate rearrangement of sections. [P. 28, (61).]

Alterations and corrections

To make a correction to a script, stick paper over the error and write the new word on top. Gummed paper strips 7 mm wide are suitable. Opaque self-adhesive ribbon is available commercially.

After you have made many corrections to a manuscript [MANUscript means HANDscript], copy out the untidiest page, using scissors and paste to avoid copying clean paragraphs. As you copy you will want to improve sentences. Rewriting is a better stimulus to making improve-
(53) ments than is mere reading. The desire to lessen the task of copying may prompt you to examine each word and to ask yourself whether it is needed. A slight laziness may even be a virtue here. The effect of making the fair copy will have been worth while. Try it; verify, or refute, the hypothesis experimentally. The rewriting scheme compels you to re-read the very parts that need it most, whereas if you have scribbled corrections across the script, you will be discouraged from re-reading the untidy stuff. Before you give the script to the typist, check that the alterations are clear. Look at p. viii. Use coloured ink for instructions.

Even if you use a word processor, I recommend you to consider the argument in the paragraph above.

Good sense

Read other people's writings critically. Even edit them – but not in library books! Improvements can usually be visualized in, and words may be deleted from, MOST papers without effect on the meaning. You may obtain amusement by collecting oddities, and this will help you to be vigilant in avoiding them in your own writing. Here are some: absent

(54)   in the solution (write 'from'); molar $CuSO_4,5H_2O$; the kind gift; at varying temperatures in a thermo*stat* (write 'various'); most probably

(55)   (i.e. $P = 1$); experiments were done in this paper; bursts of activity could be seen following doses of atropine; our records show that you do not exist; built between 1979 and 1980; cancer in rubber workers; pressure of space; drugs were given to patients dissolved in alcohol; specimens were stored in a refrigerator wrapped in Al foil; beam from a Philips machine filtered through 1 mm Cu; they were in fact not artifacts.

More desirable is the collecting of 'good stuff' [Herbert, B (11)]. When you meet good writing, study it. Try to analyse your liking for it. Then emulate it. Through attentive reading you can enlarge your vocabulary. This will help you to overcome a principal difficulty in writing:

(56)   finding the right word. When you have this difficulty (quandary, problem, doubt, perplexity, dilemma...), write various words [as here and on p. 9 (20)]. Later, you may be able to choose (select, reject, pick, exclude...) suitably. If no word fits, consult *Roget's Thesaurus* [B (17)]. If you meet a 'new' word you like, look it up in a dictionary before you use it.

Emotion and modesty in scientific writing

May I suggest that you avoid emotion in scientific papers? 'Great importance', 'significant conclusions' and similar expressions should be restrained. If you are tempted to write 'this most interesting result' ask yourself 'To whom is it most interesting?' Strunk (1959) writes 'Instead of announcing that what you are about to tell is interesting, make it so'.

If Lob published first, write 'my result agrees with that of Lob' not 'Lob confirmed my result'. You must mention your publications as necessary, but do not let the Bibliography look like a personal history.

(57)   An author who writes 'we were surprised' or 'unexpected result' admits lack of knowledge, for he who knows all can predict all. Humility is good but may not be the author's intent.

(58)   Promises should be offered only sparingly. An author who writes that an idea will be investigated may be warning you off 'his' territory.

Why omit 'other' from 'human and other animals'?

If you list arguments as 'first, ... second(ly), ...' avoid calling the last 'finally'. You can rarely be certain the subject is closed.

Of course we hope – but privately, not in a scientific paper.

Chapter Two
Preparation of the typescript and figures

(59) The script may be read by several people, usually by an editor, two referees (reviewers in the USA), a sub-editor or language corrector, the copypreparer, the printer and the proof reader. This should be sufficient reason for the preparation of clear script. Yet poorly prepared scripts are commonly submitted to editors; I have seen some that were barely legible. Even a script that looks neat may not be good from the printer's point of view. This is partly because typists' typography differs from (60) that of printers as to spacing and punctuation. [Unfortunately the typist may have had to type in that manner to pass her exams.] After the sub-editor and the copypreparer have corrected and marked the type-script it may almost resemble a MANUscript!

Therefore, for the comfort of the seven or more people who read your script, may I appeal to you to attend to the directives below? Please show them to your typist.

This is important

The typescript should have wide margins, especially at the bottom. (61) A standard left margin, say 40 mm wide, will help to ensure that pasted corrections are in alignment and that unintended indentions are avoided.

The typing should be double-spaced throughout, *including that of footnotes, notes to tables and References.* The directive in italics is often overlooked. It is not editorial pomp; the space is needed for the copy-preparer's instructions to the keyboard operator, and those instructions are usually more numerous in notes and legends than in the text. If you still think it desirable to use close spacing for any parts of the type-script, make all spelling, punctuation, units, hyphens, capitals or lower case, decimals, formulas, numbers, etc. strictly in accordance with the style of the journal. If you cannot ensure all that, then leave interlinear space for the sub-editor and copypreparer.

(62) The first line of each paragraph **should be indented**, but no more than two or three spaces. A paragraph that is not indented (for reasons of

fashion?) risks being 'run on', especially one that starts a page. This abominable non-indent fashion wastes the time of editors, who have to mark each new paragraph (NP) and who may have to turn back a page before they can decide whether an NP is desired. If you dislike indention in a script, or if the typing is done in a distant office outside your control, help the editor and his staff by marking each NP with a □.

Remember to change ug to μg and ul to μl. Thousands are missed. Ensure that symbols in legends, figures and text agree, for example 3*A* or 3*a*.

All pages must be numbered, *including the first page*, as well as the references, etc. Imagine what happens if the typescript is dropped.

The journal may request two or more copies, and it should be axiomatic that good copies be sent, yet poor photocopies and carbon copies continue to be submitted. Blurred script strains the referee's eyes because he is continually attempting – abortively – to sharpen the image by focusing. If the typewriter's ' e ' is full of fluff, please have it brushed out, for example with a toothbrush. Before you make photocopies, cut a tiny corner off each original page. Then you can identify the original and avoid making copies of copies.

Printers appreciate good copy.

Directives from a Dutch uncle

Do you think these directives are stern, strict or categorical? They are, and experience shows that they need to be. I cannot remember having yet seen a script that needed no correcting. Some scripts do not seem to have been read, in their final form, by any of the joint authors, let alone by all of them.

Bad script is unlikely to lead to rejection of a paper; but neither will it encourage the referee to read it promptly. Day [B (6)] writes that a badly typed script is immediately returned to the author. Another American editor told me that poor script may delay publication by a month.

Word division at line ends

(63) Do not split a word at the end of a line. If a hyphen appears there, the printer will usually join the parts of a word. If a hyphen is needed (as in dansyl-lysine), it is good practice to repeat the hyphen at the start of the next line. Even better, take the whole word over, because broken words interfere with reading. The lines in a typescript need not all have the same length. Do the unequal lines of this text disturb you as much as

divided words would? When a scientific paper is to be typed, the word
processor should not be instructed to divide words.

Balloons (p. viii)

(64) In the margin, type 'Table .. near here' or 'Fig. .. near here'. Draw
a ring round these and other directions to the printer about Greek
symbols, mathematics, etc. Then he will not print the directions. Such
balloons are useful in other ways too.

Cover sheet

(65) Some publishers appreciate your supplying a top sheet. On it type the
name of the journal, title of the paper, author(s), address for correspondence, running title, number of figures and number of tables.

Corrections and additions to the final copy

After a page has been retyped, check that all has been copied. If I cannot understand a passage in a typescript, I wonder whether a phrase
has been omitted. Jumps occur when a typist 'picks up' a word in error
(66) at its repeat. (See 'tape...tape' four sentences below.)

For small corrections, correct the text itself; do not make corrections
in the margin as you would on proofs. Confirm by using a balloon if
the mark is not distinct.

Corrections should not be attached with pins, clips or staples; they
embarrass the printer. If you use transparent tape let it be invisible
mending tape upon which one can write. Common self-adhesive tape
(67) should not be used. The latter, convenient though it is for authors and
secretaries, is disliked by editors and printers, comes unstuck and cannot
be written on. Flags, tails, flyleaves, turned-up pages and additions on
the back of a page cause trouble, and their contents may even be
accidentally omitted by the printer. If more than a line is to be added,
retype the page. Do not crowd the page. If there is too much for one
page, type two pages. Then re-number the pages through to the end.
Although the paper for all pages should be of uniform size, the lengths
of typescripts on pages need not be uniform. Short pages (script, not
paper) are not troublesome, but long pages are.

Word processors

Parts of what is written above do not apply when a word processor is
used. Such machines are not yet used everywhere, and even when they
are used, some authors will continue to manipulate the script physically.

The typewriter's type face

Before you buy a typewriter, look for a type style that is suitable for scientific work. Sanserif (p. xii), although fashionable, is unsuitable. If you *have* to accept sanserif and you show 'l' as part of a formula (e.g. Hl, ln) tell the printer what it means. One day, while you wait in a queue, you may like to amuse yourself by recalling possible meanings of lll; there are several.

If the product of your word processor is a dot-matrix print-out, look at the script critically before you send it to a journal. If the legibility is indifferent, the editor is entitled to return your script.

Books on the preparation of printers' copy

Editors and others who prepare the copy for the printer will find useful information in *Copy-editing* by J. Butcher and in BS 5261. *The Oxford Dictionary for Writers & Editors* is especially useful to editors and sub-editors. These books are described in Chapter Seven, B (13) onwards.

Drawing the diagrams for reproduction

(68) Draw diagrams at least twice the *dimensions* of the desired printed version. (If the directives say twice the *size*, that is probably an error.) Such enlargement demands thick lines, perhaps thicker than seem necessary to your eye. Curves should be more prominent than axes. Ensure that lines in different diagrams will appear equally thick, for example by using the same scale for all drawings. Insert the 'points' of a graph in ink. Sketch the curve first in pencil, free-hand or against a flexible rule. You can then erase the curve for re-drawing without losing the points. Or you may be able to calculate the line of best fit. The Biochemical Society's *Instructions* [B (2)] give detailed directions on drawing graphs.

The camera operator likes drawings to be on smooth card, bristol board or good quality tracing paper, but graph paper is usually acceptable provided its lines are faint blue. Graph paper helps one to keep drawings of apparatus square. To transfer a diagram to Bristol board, fix the former on the latter, then prick through principal points with a needle. The tiny holes provide a template for your drawing. They will be inked over, and should cause no trouble.

Line drawings are reproduced by an all-or-none process. So draw your lines densely black; faint blue lines, pencillings, etc. may not appear in the printing plate. Deletions can be made with adhesive paper.

Thus you can make a continuous curve dotted or dashed by sticking narrow strips of gummed paper over it at intervals. Printed-pattern paper can be cut to shape and stuck over particular areas to make them hatched (shaded).

Words or numerals should be written on a transparent detachable overlay. Many printers can insert such lettering professionally, but this possibility should be checked with the editor. An inexperienced draughtsman has difficulty in making the letters of suitable size. Examine a journal with author-drawn letters and you will see that unsuitable lettering spoils a picture. If you draw your own letters or apply pressure-
(69) sensitive transfers, use lower-case letters; they are more legible than capitals. [See 'Legibility of print', B (1).] Label each curve if possible; seeking explanations in the legend is tiresome for the reader. The labelling must be brief, so as not to dominate the graphs. If there is not room for words on each curve, that may be because there are too many curves in the figure. Hers (1984) recommends the use of open ('empty') symbols for control curves; he also makes other good suggestions.

Draw a magnifier bar with scale value *on the picture*; then, if the picture is reduced, the bar is reduced too. A magnification number in the legend is unsatisfactory on several counts.

(70) **Journey's end for the script**

If you write many papers or a book, visit a printing works. You may then see what can be done and what is typographically costly. If you are shown examples of good and bad copy, you will see that the above disquisition on the preparation of a typescript is not too detailed. Further, you should see why alterations at the proof stage are expensive.

Chapter Three
Speaking at scientific meetings

Craftsmanship in speaking at meetings

Most scientists attend conferences and listen to talks by other scientists. Sometimes a speaker so enthrals listeners that they enjoy hearing him talk about his work and they listen intently. On the other hand, a speaker may be so dull, ill-prepared or inaudible that listeners fail to follow what he says.

Between such speakers are all the others, most of whom could deliver a better talk if they were helped. Some speakers may not even realize that they could improve their performance after reading about speaking. Many conference attenders have told me they have suffered while striving to listen to such speakers. Because I have suffered too, I have been 'inspired' (if that be the right word), by the performance of not-so-good speakers, to write this chapter. Books on lecturing exist, but scientists are too busy to read them. Perhaps they can find time to glance through this chapter or at least to read about empty words and visual aids.

Bad manners

If a scientist gives a talk without taking care to make it easily understandable, that is bad manners. This chapter offers a code of conduct. Rule one is that a person should speak only if he has something to say, not solely to justify his expenses.

Direct style

Part of what I have written is in the imperative. This is because the imperative allows the most vigorous and most readable style. I write as though I am speaking to you because one day I may be listening to you.

Title of your talk

Look at a list of talks; some titles tell us what the talk will be about, some do not. Ensure that yours does that.

(71)

How to begin

Listeners do not always take in the first sentence of a talk; they are 'tuning in'. So do not start with crucial information. If you have to tell us what an honour it is to be invited..., that can be your opening, but limit it to one sentence. If you do not need that opening, look at the back of the room and ask 'Can you hear me?' I have done that; it works.

Now begin.

What to talk about

Please tell us
1 why you did this work;
2 how you did it;
3 what you found;
4 what you think it means.

Thank your audience (five words); then stop.

A scientific talk should not be prepared in the form of a written paper. You are telling us of your recent discovery, so the first three parts make up the necessary prelude to your main Message in part 4. In a short communication, the first two of those parts should not take up much time. In a written paper, a scientist must so describe his method that another can repeat the experiments. In a talk, we must assume that your method was suitable; a description of the principle of the method should suffice. Anybody who wishes to pursue your experiments can speak to you afterwards.

Part 3 should take most of your allotted time. You have to tell us enough results to support your conclusion, but you must simplify them. The results must not be cluttered with statistical details. Just tell us the averages, for example from your experiments with and without treatments, and their statistical significance; we have to trust that your calculations are correct. A graph is more easily understood than is any but the simplest table; the more results you have the more complicated is the table, but the better the graph.

Now tell us your Conclusion (part 4). This is the part we have come to hear. So you must do all you can to convey this part clearly. Let there be no distraction: for example, turn off the projector; do not rustle your notes. If there is an interruption beyond your control and you see people looking away from you, tell us 'I'll say that again'. Your courage will be admired.

Verbal delivery

Let us now consider how you can make yourself heard and understood.

A good speaker looks at his audience, not at the bench (or lectern), wallboard ('black'board) or screen. He holds up his head and speaks to the people at the back of the room. Then those at the front should hear too.

Do not read your 'talk'. If you read, you may go too fast or speak in a monotone; you will lower your head, compress your lungs, and perhaps become inaudible. If you *have* to read a passage, hold the book high.

Notes as prompter

Prepare notes and, if they help you, use them. There is nothing shameful about that. Notes are better in the form of headings than of sentences: then you can refer to them with a glance. The lettering should be large, clear and well spaced, in lower-case letters, not capitals. Make the notes on cards so that you can carry them if you walk to the wallboard or elsewhere. Number the cards. My (paper) notes were once blown to the floor by the overhead projector's fan. How glad I was that they were numbered. Now I use cards.

On the top page of notes it is helpful to write a check-list of items to be taken into the lecture hall, e.g. clock, mask for the projector, coloured markers, pen, books, exhibits....

If you have slides, apparatus, specimens, transparencies to exhibit, signal them with numbers on your notes – *in colour*. The audience is not well impressed by: 'Oh yes – I should have shown this earlier'. The numbers on the reminders should tally with the numbers written on the items.

Some speakers, not knowing what to do with their hands, put them into pockets. This is inelegant. Notes can help, by occupying your hands.

Stage fright

If you have delivered many talks or lectures, please skip this section.

However, if you are a novice, you may wonder what you can do to overcome nervousness. *Most* people are nervous immediately before, or even during, their first public talk. With practice in speaking to groups of people, you will find that the nervousness diminishes. One man's knees shook so violently when he stood on the platform that he had to hold the table. Several talks later he felt only a trace of nervousness before speaking and none during his talks. So people need practice; and the smaller their first audience the easier it is for them. This is one – but not the only – reason why every laboratory or institute should have a tea club at which each research worker tells his colleagues what he is doing. If your institute does not yet have a club, perhaps you can initiate one. [P. 1 (3).]

Starting with a large audience can be devastating, as the following incident shows. The television broadcast had begun. The next speaker was awaiting his turn. Suddenly he said 'Oh, my car!' and ran out. The producer assumed the man had suddenly remembered parking his car where he should not. He did not return....

One precaution you can take against stage fright is to ensure that your notes cannot go astray. You could (not many people would) make a copy of your notes to keep in a pocket. The knowledge that everything is in order gives you confidence.

If you let it be seen that you have not prepared your talk, and if you fail to speak coherently, the audience will not like you. However, if the audience senses that you have taken trouble but are stage struck, that audience will be sympathetic. Knowledge of such sympathy encourages a speaker, and his nervousness diminishes.

Importance of deliberate speech

Speak so s l o w l y that it seems almost absurd. There are good reasons. When we stand, with knees shaking, before an audience, adrenaline speeds us up, and we do not realize how fast we speak. During a lecture I was giving about speaking, I asked the audience to observe its pulse rate. The average was 65 beats per min; mine was 130. This was taken as evidence of my speed-up. When the experiment was repeated a dozen lectures later, my rate was only 75 beats per min. So I had to give a false value to make my point. I had become adapted to lecturing.

A maximal rate for speech is 100 words per minute. So a 10-min talk should be kept below 1000 words.

Rehearse your talk – to a colleague or to a tape recorder. Use a clock. Remember, he who exceeds his time is a thief. He is also unwise, because a strict chairperson may stop him before he has uttered his Conclusion. Ask your critic not only to time you but also to tell you if you have distracting mannerisms.

Empty words and non-words

If you are to speak slowly, yet have much to say, how can you resolve the dilemma? Contribute to a solution by uttering necessary words *only*.

That means, aim at a high signal-to-noise ratio. Waste no words, for example, over telling us you have not the time to say everything. Non-information of that sort irritates the audience.

Omit 'empty words' such as: very; in this context; quite; it has to be pointed out here that; as a matter of fact; the whole point is. . . .

Avoid tautology: repeated again; pooled together; three different kinds; still remains; supplemented with additional salt. Obvious? Yes, but these double sayings do creep in.

This striving for economy also means start sentences without 'Anderm', an irritating non-word, or 'Well'. When you listen to an interview on television or radio, compare the interviewer's speech with that of the untrained interviewee. If you find yourself counting the times the latter says 'you know', 'that sort of thing' or 'I mean' perhaps that will stimulate you to listen to yourself on a tape recorder, identify your personal in-fill word (or non-word), then train yourself to forgo it. That is difficult, but it can be done; it *must* be done if you are to 'capture' your audience.

May I entreat you, please, to read that last paragraph again?

If you speak deliberately, that will give you time to choose your words with care. You will then be able to offer more information per unit time than can he who talks fast but interjects 'you see' or 'as it were' and joins phrases intoalmostinterminablesentencespaddedwith empty words and noise.

Hackneyed phrases

Clichés, such as 'tip of the iceberg' and 'acid test', should be avoided.

Questions from the audience

Because you cannot include all experimental details, you may be asked about them during the discussion. You may also be asked critical questions about your Conclusion. Anticipate questions, and be prepared to answer them succinctly.

Verbal style

We, your listeners, prefer that you 'talk' to us rather than deliver a formal speech. This calls for a simple style. Here are suggestions.

In general, use short sentences. But they must not all be very short or the delivery will be jerky. A pleasing sentence usually has two main verbs, but an occasional short sentence can be used for emphasis. (See the next paragraph.) If an interpreter is present, remember that he can translate compact sentences more easily than long ones.

Please finish every sentence.

Pronunciation

Try to remember M'Fline all the time you are speaking. [P. x (1).] Perhaps you are he. Articulate each word distinctly for him, and pronounce, not swallow, even the unaccented syllables at ends of words. Then your own nationals will hear you too.

Technical words should be pronounced unmistakably. For example, pronounce the y in methyl and in benzyl as in 'by', even if it is not your local custom to do so.

People from Britain or from North America, when speaking in the other place, should remember that not only does pronunciation differ, but different words may be used. [Fume cupboard, hood; earth, ground....] Therefore, misunderstanding must be forestalled.

If English is not your native language, try to find someone who will check your pronunciation.

Keywords

Your talk may depend upon our hearing a particular word. When you utter that word it may be drowned by a local cough or scrape. Then the audience loses the thread. Therefore, write such KEYWORDS on the wallboard and point to each as needed. The shorter the word the more important this gesture. On your notes mark each keyword in colour as a reminder. I tried to follow a talk by Dr M'Fline; he spoke his keyword many times, always mispronounced it, but never wrote it. For me, at least, his message failed.

Partial deafness

Perhaps as many as one in five of your audience has a hearing defect.[1] Many such people are unaware of their partial deafness (PD). The diminished ability to hear is not evenly spread across the auditory 'spectrum': usually the loss is more severe in the higher than in the lower frequencies, although there may be selective loss at lower

[1] Note the absence of 'every'. An author should only write 'one in every five' if he actually means that.

frequencies. Therefore, the use of an amplifier may not help. What *does* help people with PD is clear and deliberate enunciation. Because that cannot be given in rapid speech, here is one more reason for you to

speak slowly.

A person with PD can understand best if he can see a speaker's face, especially the lips. So there is good reason for you to stand in the light and to look at the audience. Dress neither over-formally nor outrageously; be tidy, so that you are easy to look at.

Words

Use short words where you can: start, not commence; try, not endeavour; often, not frequently.... An uncommon word may express a *writer's* meaning exactly. There are examples in this book. A reader can, if he wishes, consult a dictionary about an unfamiliar word. Because a listener cannot do that in a lecture, a *speaker* should avoid such words.

Vogue words, too, should be avoided, unless they are really suitable. Examples are: focus, perspective, restructured, breakthrough, situation. On p. 42 space is offered in which you may add other words and thereby discharge some of your feelings.

'Constantly' is constantly used (as it is here) to mean no more than 'often'. 'Continually', 'repeatedly', 'regularly', or even 'sometimes', may better represent the desired meaning. Reserve 'constant' for unchanging. Say 'constantly changing' only if you mean just that. Only say 'invariably' if you mean always; even better, say always. A speaker who says that bad weather constantly [or invariably] interfered with observations means annoyingly often, and he implies that the Law of Exasperation was at work.

'Localized' is sometimes used for 'located'. The latter means that something is situated, or was found, there; the former means it is *only* there – the longer word is restrictive.

'Relatively' and 'comparatively' should only be used if there are things to be compared. Alone, these words have only limited meaning. So has 'a fraction of'.

'While' should be restricted to its temporal meaning; try 'whereas', 'although' or even 'and'. Similarly, 'because' sometimes betters 'since'. Did an author really mean '*A* began an experiment while *B* finished it'?

When you are speaking, do not use foreign words for words that already exist in English, even though you might use them when you write. [P. 15 (32)].

Contemporary terms

Be up to date over units and technical terms. Young listeners who have to 'translate' archaic names may 'lose' your next sentence. Such terms as condenser (for capacitor) or normal solutions may not be familiar to those who have recently left school.

Courtesy requires attention to detail

You may think I am a fusspot and that these details do not interest ordinary people. But we are not ordinary people. We are special people. You would not trouble to read about speaking were you not a Special Person. Therefore, I hope you will campaign with me for better scientific talks.

Pronouns it and I

Speakers often say 'it' as a stand-in for a word so distant that we may not remember it. Be safe: repeat it. [Do you see what I mean? the 'it' should have been 'the word'.] Listeners cannot 'refer back' as readers can.

The word 'I' need not be avoided altogether. If you feel enthusiastic about your work, try to convey your enthusiasm to us. An occasional (72) 'I' helps, although too many are bad. Of course, you will not call yourself 'we' – unless you are royalty, an editor, pregnant, or the spokesperson of a team.

Visual aids

If you use a projector, let your tables be truly simple. Never display more results than the argument needs. Tables from your published papers may not be suitable for the screen. So, please, *make your tables especially for the occasion.* Project the most crowded of your slides in an empty lecture room. If, from the back of the room, you cannot read the display, remake the slide. If a speaker shows an overloaded table on the screen, or on the wallboard, listeners wonder whether to study the table or listen to the speaker. They may try both and in the event do neither, so that the speaker might have achieved more without the display.

If you make slides, read what Norris (1978) says about their preparation. His essay is excellent. If an indicator of magnification is needed, show a measured bar. The ' × 1000' becomes meaningless on the screen.

Before you use an episcope in public, check whether what it projects is visible from the back of the hall.

If you use a hand-held illuminated arrow, switch it off when it is not needed. Some speakers wave it about in a distracting manner or even, unknowingly, point it at the audience.

Switch off the projector immediately you have finished with it, even though you may need it later. (See Appendix, p. 43). The audience should pay attention to what you are saying now, not to what you displayed minutes ago; and they should not be dazzled by a bright empty screen. Write a reminder on your notes.

Some speakers use slides to project their notes on to the screen, and talk around them. This is undesirable on three counts: the room has to be darkened; the audience reads ahead; and the speaker tends to speak to the screen. These objections vanish if an overhead projector is used, together with a mask, although some speakers tend to speak to the projector.

Overhead projector

An overhead projector has advantages over a slide projector (diascope). (Appendix, p. 43.)

Before you prepare transparencies, take a white card and draw lines, about 20 mm apart, across it. If you lay a transparent film on the card, the lines will help you to arrange your words neatly. As a compositor says: it's the arrangement of the white space that's important. Prepare your transparencies with permanent ink, then use suitable dense water-soluble ink for numbering the transparencies as well as for marking during your talk. After the talk or lecture, your marks and the number may be washed off, but the original writing remains for re-use. Write with bold clear lettering, NOT IN CAPITALS. [P. 32 (69).] Typewritten characters, unless enlarged, are too small. We are not entertained by the remark 'I suppose you can't see these numbers'.

Immediately *before* you project, place a mask of thick paper over the display; then move the mask down to uncover what you want the audience to see as you speak. Do not first display the whole, *then* cover it; that is discourteous.

Microphone and loudspeakers

Should you use a speech amplifier? If you have a strong voice and will speak up – no. Even the best systems give some distortion; and your freedom may be restricted. If you must face the screen or wallboard, an amplifier may be advisable.

Light relief

Should you make a humorous remark or tell a funny story? Yes, if it be relevant, brief, witty and dignified. Not otherwise. Favourable response from an audience will dispel nervousness and help you to speak better. And we shall listen alertly in the hope of more. Perhaps you can recall an incident from a previous lecture, or you may have seen a title worth quoting such as 'Prevention of sudden recurrent death' (new jargon, perhaps?).

This chapter does not tell everything

I have made suggestions. You can probably make others. Here is space for them.

You may like to read Kenny (1983) on public speaking.

Formal lectures

My intention in writing this chapter (coming as it were, from the body of the audience) was to appeal to those giving short talks. A graph of listeners' comprehension against time shows a fall within 10 min. So my points about good speech and sensible delivery for short talks are relevant to 50-min talks too.

Directive for lulling an audience to sleep

Wear a dark suit and conventional tie; turn down the lights;
close the curtains (drapes); display a crowded slide and leave
it in place; stand still; *read* your paper without looking up;
read steadily with no marked changes in cadence; show no
pictures; use grandiloquent words and long sentences.

Appendix on projectors

We are told not to switch projectors (any kind) off and on because that is bad for the lamp. Switching need not be bad if a thermistor has been fitted; every projector should have one.

(73) Overhead projectors have several merits in comparison with slide projectors, including the following. The room need not be darkened. Projection is under the speaker's control. The speaker can face the audience. A display can be unmasked gradually. Displays can be developed during a talk. Transparencies prepared beforehand can be written on during a talk. Insertion upside-down is obviated. Transparencies can be prepared, or modified, without photography and therefore immediately before a talk if needed. Colours are easily included. One transparency can be superimposed on another. Large transparencies are easy for interested parties to examine after a talk. If a speaker prepares his own transparencies and writes in large lettering, he is less likely to put too much on them than if he has someone else make slides from typewritten copy. [See p. 25 (53).]

Against this dozen merits of overhead projectors there are some demerits, but most of them could be overcome by better design of the projector and of its immediate environment. Often the overhead projector is placed on a table or trolley that is too low for the speaker: he has to bend over, which is bad on several counts; and he may be dazzled as he straightens up. If you are able to do so, ask to see the projector before your talk and ask to have it raised. I have done that a few times. I sometimes wonder, has that trolley's designer (a short person?) or the head of the institute, ever used the projector? A speaker needs more than a narrow lectern. A flat-topped bench is needed to provide space for transparencies and other items. In some lecture rooms the projector is sited out of reach of the speaker; much of the merit of the projector is then lost.

A quiet fan is desirable. A curved mirror might be designed to lessen trapezoidal aberration.

If instruction on the siting and use of an overhead projector were good, perhaps fewer people would resist using this admirable machine.

Chapter Four
Addressed to those for whom English is a foreign language

Particular errors occur in scripts written by those whose first language is not English. The errors make the difference between foreign 'engelish' and idiomatic English. Errors of idiom distract a reader. You want the reader to be attracted, not distracted. This chapter is intended to help you to achieve that.

Words

Certain errors often occur in translation. Sometimes this is because an English word (control, eventual, sensible) resembles a foreign word that has another meaning. Other troublesome words are discussed below.

acknowledge. You may acknowledge receiving a gift, but you thank the donor. One does not acknowledge a colleague for help; one thanks him.

also commonly occurs in a wrong place; the best place is usually before the main verb. So does 'already'. The editor may delete the words because they are not always needed in the English translation.

both. 'Both wires were not hot' leaves it uncertain whether one of them was hot. Write 'neither wire was hot', if both were cold.

control, the verb, does not mean count, measure or observe. Control means govern, maintain or limit a variable such as a rate of flow or a potential difference. Measure, check or monitor may be what the writer means. Control, the noun, is well understood and needs no explanation.

could occurs too often. 'We could see' or 'were able to see' tells only of your ability to see. If you actually saw, say so. 'We saw' is brief and definite. In 'the friction could be too great' perhaps the writer meant '...may have been'.

demonstrate is often written where another word would be better. The word has various meanings, the most usual being physically to display or show something happening. 'Nob reports that leaves of some trees contain gold' is more cautious than 'Nob has demonstrated...'. 'Show' is less grandiloquent than demonstrate, but is not always suitable. Write 'the results show' [not demonstrate]; but write 'Cob has found' rather than 'Cob has shown' because he was writing about his experiments, not showing them. 'Table 3 shows' is better than 'It can be seen in Table 3'. Usually, 'it has been demonstrated that' may be omitted; if you write about another person's observation, write in the present tense and give the reference; the meaning should then be understood and the five words are not needed. If you saw red grains among predominantly green grains, write that they were seen rather than demonstrated.

describe is a transitive verb. You may describe a method or an apparatus. But 'Blob has described that chopped straw makes good fodder' is not good English. Write that he claims, states, writes or reports.

dosis is not in common use; write 'dose'.

eventually does not mean maybe. The event *will* happen – ultimately.

experience should not be written for experiment.

filtrated should be filtered.

insignificant, which means unimportant, should not be used in statistics. Write 'were not statistically significant' and quote the P value, or write non-significant. If you have no P value, you may write 'negligible'.

know should not be used in the sense of to provide knowledge. 'The fossils were studied to know...' is not good. Write 'we studied the fossils to find out...'.

obtain means acquire, be given. Manipulations provide (not obtain) material.

quantitate is not a word. You may quantify the effects though that is a grandiloquent word for measure.

registrated is not a word; observations are usually recorded rather than registered.

resorption should not be written for absorption, except in the sense of re-absorption, or for the special case of resorption of a foetus, limb or other part originally produced by the body.

respectively. In 'we cleaned the sherds and tiles, respectively' the word respectively is not needed, but is needed in 'we cleaned the sherds and tiles with water and oil, respectively'. Change 'blue respectively red' to 'blue and red, respectively', and do not abbreviate to resp.

since. Write 'seven years ago' not 'since seven years'.

supposed may be bettered by believed, for example, in 'Birds are believed to have evolved from dinosaurs'.

Idiomatic English

Some common errors of idiom will now be discussed.

using, or other verb, written without an operator, is the commonest

error. Authors of all nationalities make the error, which is condemned
by writers of style books. See Dangling participle, p. 9 (21).

'This permits to do that' needs an operator after permits; for example
us.

'Powder was added and stirred' is not good English. Write 'Powder
was added and the mixture was stirred'.

The abbreviation a.o. is not in common use, but 'etc.' is. The abbreviation for number is no. not nr. [P. 15 (31).]

Things compared must be comparable. 'Growth was similar to the
controls' needs 'that in' before 'the'. 'Lymphocytes from treated
patients were larger than untreated patients' needs 'those from' after
'than'. 'Resonances in pipes were unlike rods' needs 'those in' before
'rods'.

Spelling

Certain words are commonly misspelt: occurred, subtract, oxidation,
centrifuged, homogeneous, synthesize, desiccate, naphthol, phthalic,
saccharide.

Use of a dictionary to check meanings of English words

You may find a wanted word in your Spandanese–Engels dictionary.
Next, back-check the English word in your Engels–Spandanese dictionary. Then consult an English dictionary (Chapter Seven) to confirm that
the word is what you want. This procedure will help you to avoid
writing spatial cubicle when you mean spacious, vaulted caterpillar when
you mean arched, favourite for favourable, or sensible for sensitive, or
that the animals' diet was spiked with vitamins. You might be em-
barrassed were you to see, in print, that you had written permissiveness
for permittivity.

While you are using the English dictionary to check the word, note
how it is pronounced.

Speaking at conferences

Unless you have often conversed in English, try to find someone who
will check your pronunciation. If you empha'size incorr'ect sylla'bles the
audience has to interpret words and may lose a sentence during the time
it takes to do that. I have lost many such sentences.

International conventions

Use the international decimal point (0.6 g) for papers in English unless your publisher prefers the comma (0,6 g). Write 100 000 not 100.000 or 100,000 if you mean one hundred thousand.

Encouragement

For your comfort may I add that Englishmen, too, find it difficult to write good English?

When you visit England or another English-speaking country, or when you watch and listen to television from such a country, you may be appalled by the poor quality of parts of the speech you hear. You probably have a better knowledge of grammar than do the natives! You may even be able to help to keep up the quality of what is now the International Language, especially when you become an editor. I hope you will do that; I have known several overseas scientists who have done so.

Chapter Five
An appeal to North Americans

There are more of you than there are of us. So you are now the Trustees of English, the International Language. Sad to say, not all of you are taking your trusteeship seriously.

One language

English, *at its best*, is much the same on both sides of the Atlantic.

True, we spell some words differently, but we mostly understand one another. Several of these words are spelt more phonetically in the USA than in Britain. One day perhaps we shall have a unified spelling....

True, too, several words for food, transport and domestic items are different; but in science the differences are few – at present.

Please understand, I do not suggest that where American English and British English differ, the British version is always the better. Rather, I suggest that the form more easily understandable by M'Fline [p. x (1)] is the better.

In this chapter, I shall discuss some of the features of American English that may cause trouble for Dr M'Fline. Other chapters deal with troubles that may arise in the writing or speaking of English by people of *any* nationality.

Grammar

A characteristic of English is that the grammar is simpler than that of many languages. People abroad, many of whom speak a language having complex grammar, learn English grammatically. So when M'Fline meets an example of bad grammar in a published work, or at a conference, he may be confused.

On behalf of those abroad who use English, I appeal to you to persuade emergent authors to follow such rules of grammar that exist, and to punctuate carefully.

In English, the same word can sometimes be used as a noun (*tin*), an adjective (*tin* can) and a verb (to *tin* the copper wire). But this grammatical freedom should not be extended to every word. For example, consider the phrase 'a book was authored'. Why not say 'written'? 'Authored' gives no special shade of meaning.

Where a verb is needed but none exists, it is practical to use a noun (to program, to chromatograph); but 'to gift' (mineral samples were gifted by Dr Fob) is unnecessary.

Adjectives are sometimes used as nouns (all time high) or as adverbs ('sure' for surely); *real bad is that*.

Hopefully is often used ambiguously. Were I to write 'Hopefully you will agree with some statements' that would mean you (not I) hope.

Complex adjectival phrases

What Woodford (1970) calls stacked modifiers (SM) are almost interminable and at times barely comprehensible noun adjective and modifier groups (as is that one). German immigrants are believed to have brought SM into American English; now SM are being re-exported to Europe.

Consider 'voluntary human kidney donor research institution personnel'. A reader has to read six words before he realizes the writer means people not kidneys. The reader of 'barley root tip cell chromosome aberrations' sees five false nouns before finding the real noun. The five checks or hold-ups that require quick re-thinking tire the brain. The phrase would be better as 'chromosomal aberrations in root-tip cells of barley'.

The US journal *Science* carried correspondence on 'adjective noun use tendency'. Hildebrand (1983) gave examples of shockingly cumbersome phrases, and suggested that 'of' should be used to obviate them. On the other hand, Baer (1983) disliked 'measurement of the angle of the joint of the ankle' and thought 'ankle-joint angle measurement' was better. Better still would have been 'measurement of the ankle-joint angle'.

So far as practicable, SM should be avoided in writing and in speech. [See p. 8 (17).]

Future tense

Students of English abroad learn that shall and will are used formally for the future tense, but that 'to be going to' is usual in speech. In the USA – and, alas, in Britain too – the 'going to' is corrupted to the inelegant 'gunner' (usually spelt, unphonetically, 'gonna').

Americanizations

An Americanism that makes editors wince is the making of words by
adding -ize, -ism or ization. Examples are prioritized, delogarithmization
and summarization. If you see such words in a printed paper, perhaps
you will try to persuade colleagues and your research students to abstain
from such 'manufacturization'.

Long words

M'Fline should not be encouraged, by example, to use ponderous words
where simple words are adequate. Here are examples for you to consider: 'subsequently to' is a grandiloquent way of writing 'after';
methodology rarely betters method; enzymatic is less elegant than
enzymic; detoxification is no improvement on detoxication, or sonifi-
cation on sonication; are experimental animals killed, or sacrificed?

In some US journals, the 'al' has been been dropped from physiological, symmetrical, serological and other words; so can other needless
syllables be dropped too – for example, those mentioned above?

Caring Americans ARE concerned about the trend

In case you think I am biased, let me remind you that authors of
American books on writing also dislike the bad features discussed here.

Houp & Pearsall, in their excellent book [B (4)], give a list of pom-
posities to be avoided. If you have not read their Chapter 8, you have
missed (out on) a treat.

Day [B (6)] instructs scientists – firmly – to use short words.

Woodford's (1970) piece on stacked modifiers, mentioned above,
deserves study. He wrote it in the USA.

Nicholson's *American English Usage* [B (9)], though out of print,
deserves to be in print. She argues eloquently against careless writing;
her own prose provides pleasant reading.

Holman (1962) writes 'Inelegant writing may charm the writer, but...
offends the reader'. He quotes several abominations, including 'We
horizontalized the patient ... and decholecystectomized him'.

An American scientist (David E. Green, later to become a professor
in the University of Wisconsin) instructed me in scientific writing, when
I was a research student. He taught me, among other things, only to
write an 'it' that could easily be related to a noun. He was careful to
say 'I have to' not 'I gotta'. I learned much from him.

Editors of several US journals are evidently particular about English.
Articles in *Scientific American*, for example, as well as papers in various
other journals, are (mostly) noticeably well written and edited.

The annual Gobbledegook Award is an American institution.

Obviously, then, some Americans do care, and care very much, about the future of the language of science. Alas, they are not a majority. If more US scientists wrote as one of you (Strunk, 1959) recommends, this chapter might be unnecessary.

Export

You may point out that long words, complex modifiers and wrong use of words are found in European writings and elsewhere. True; but (*a*) not so often as in the USA, (*b*) they may have come from the USA, and (*c*) that is no defense for their perpetuation in US journals that will be sold abroad.

When Americans export words they should be careful to ensure that what they export is good. The export may be unwitting, but it occurs nonetheless, through journals, conferences, television.... People abroad copy what Americans write and say – the bad as well as the good. 'Prior to', for example, is becoming common in foreign writing; 'effect' and 'affect' are interchanged; and 'thus' is used abroad where hence, so, therefore or evidently might be better. So please take care over these and other words.

In chromatography, a column of adsorbent, sometimes called the bed, is held in a tube. The tube is the support; it is not the column. In the USA, the word column is used for either. This confusion has been exported; so when a writer in any country states the length of a column, the reader cannot always tell whether the length is that of the container or the contents; it is the latter that matters.

Corn, a general term, means grain or cereal. In the Americas, corn usually means Indian corn or maize; in wheat-growing countries, corn may mean wheat. So, when a scientist speaks or writes about maize, or maize oil used in diets, he (she) should give it that name and the Latin name (*Zea mays*), because some of his listeners or readers may be foreign.

Homonyms, words with various meanings

Formerly, to fix meant to make secure. In the USA, 'fix' is used for many meanings including mend, destroy, mix (a drink), prepare and several others. This peculiarity confuses foreigners whose lexicon tells them fix means fasten. Does 'he fixed the blockage in the apparatus' mean that he made it permanent or that he cleared, i.e. *un*fixed it? 'Genetic lesions were fixed' has the *opposite* meaning of genetic lesions were repaired. When 'repair' is ultimately lost, perhaps the word will persist only as jargon in molecular biology!

The use of a word for divers meanings, for which words already exist, might be called 'homonymization', an unpleasant word for an unnecessary process.

Most of the words that have so far taken over the meanings of other words are used generally rather than for science. However, unless the Trustees are vigilant, this 'homonymization' will continue to invade scientific communication too, as some words have already done, including 'due to' for owing to [p. 12 (30)] and localization for location [p. 39].

The adjective alter'nate refers to a happening to one thing *then* the other; alter'native implies a choice of one *or* the other. To al'ternate is the verb. Electric current that alternates is called AC; DC is an alternative to AC. In an AC circuit, each pole is alternately positive then negative and so on.

Transportation was the action of transporting, and transport is the means used for the transportation. In the USA the longer word is now used for both meanings. An engineer, writing a review paper on mechanical transport, might need both meanings....

'Practical' and practicable are sometimes interchanged. The wearing of goggles in a laboratory is practicable in the sense that one is able to wear them, but vizors are more practical because they are ventilated.

A referee is one who reads a paper and makes recommendations to the editor. A reviewer writes reviews for publication. There are two words for two meanings. Why abandon one?

Animals are given, or fed on, a diet, not fed the diet. One may feed an animal, but one cannot feed a diet. A US author 'fed a piscivorous diet'. He probably meant that his animals, not his diets, were fish eaters.

If 'bred' is written for 'mated', readers outside the USA may not understand. Mated is understood internationally to mean that males and females were brought together for reproduction. Bred has other meanings. After many selections and matings [or cross-pollinations] a new strain of animal [or plant] may be 'bred'.

'Watershed' and 'catchment area' are two terms with two meanings. Why then is the first word used for both meanings and the second suppressed?

In Europe, stones and rocks have different meanings. By using 'rocks' for both, you may be losing a useful distinction. If you say 'rocks', a European might not know that you mean [his] 'stones'; he thinks of rocks as being bigger than stones and usually fixed to the world.

The abbreviation 'gas' may confuse a foreign engineer who thinks of gasoline as a liquid. In technical journals perhaps the abbreviation should be avoided.

Ensure and insure have two meanings, two spellings and two

pronunciations. Only 'ensure' (to make sure) is likely to be needed in scientific communication, but do you not think we should keep the separate spellings?

Practice (noun) and practise (verb) are two words in Britain. Has something perhaps been lost by the recognizing of only one spelling in the USA? A similar question might be asked about licence and license or tyre and tire, but not about advice and advise.

With words being 'sacrificed' or made to double up, poor M'Fline hopes his Spandanese–Engels lexicon will not be rendered out of date faster than the publisher can cope with change. In a US dictionary, you may find some of these alternative meanings of given words. Dictionaries do not instruct, but only report on usage. For M'Fline's sake, please do not provide them with more material for homonymization.

Words beyond recall

Maybe it is too late to save pistol, stones, mend, locate, owing to, candy and other words with specific meanings. However, if the decay continues, your grandchildren may not be able to read and understand Mark Twain's books. Does that sadden you?

Of course you cannot be expected to give up established idioms (this moment in time, face 'up to' a problem, meet 'up with' a colleague) and words (gas, institutionalized, make (for arrive at)). Nevertheless, various examples are given in this chapter to remind you of the trend and to reinforce my appeal to you not to let *other* confusing usages or lengthy phrases become established. A professor at the University of Minnesota reminded me that you cannot *reverse* the flow of the Mississippi. In view of your other engineering feats, I believe you could *control* the flow.

How large is your vocabulary?

An ample vocabulary is a necessity for every scientist, although the meaning of ample here may be arguable.

Would you like to do an experiment? Open a dictionary; on one page, count the words whose meanings you know; turn to other pages, then count...; divide your total by the number of pages you examined; multiply this average by the number of pages in the book. Then compare your grand total with the half million words in the language. I have done that; the result was humbling.

American words

Sad to say, we have dropped some Elizabethan words that you have
kept (gotten, fall, closet...). Faucet is hardly known in Europe, although
it betters 'tap' because the latter has various meanings.

Nevertheless, the world does know many of your words. OK and
radio are universal. Scientist, hindsight and blurb are in common use.
Opine (though many hate it and only few say it) is more apt than guess
or figure, which do not mean believe. The world knows that a wrench is
a spanner, even though the former hints at cruelty to nuts.

American wordsmiths have invented these words. So why do they not
invent others when they are needed instead of using existing words for
new meanings? Alternatively, since we accept so many of your words,
why not accept some of ours?

The lack of understanding of each other's words is curious. 'Fish &
chips' has been ubiquitous for so long in Britain that it may be considered the national dish, and the word chips has been in use since
before potato crisps were invented. Why then are Britain's chips
described as French fries? Because the latter are thinner? They are not
always. The term has even come to Britain. This is an example of the
(mainly one-way) migration of words.

Words that give no information

Scientists of all nationalities write and say what Houp & Pearsall
[B (4)] call empty words. The use of certain of these words was, until
recently, peculiar to North America. 'Right' is an example; in what way
does 'right now' differ from now?

The superfluous 'right' and other words (up to, up with, out on...)
are right now invading 'up' Europe and are being uttered in scientific
talks. The Trustees should set a good example by leaving them out,
unless a special shade of meaning is desired.

Other words to be used with restraint include such vogue words as
basically and exotic.

Because Americans invent such pithy phrases as 'Tuesday through
Friday' is it not odd that they write 'in the neighborhood of' for 'about'
and 'in the event that' for 'if'?

Speaking abroad

If you come to Britain to talk to us, please remember that we speak a
strange dialect of your language. So help us by enunciating every word
distinctly. When you take part in an international congress or in a

television program for export, try to speak slowly. If you have so much to tell that you must race, you will not achieve your objective if listeners cannot understand all you say. To gain time, use short words and utter no needless words.

Please take especial care over the pronunciation of technical words when you speak to people overseas. Both metal mercury and methyl mercury are poisons, but they act differently. In a television program a speaker pronounced metal as meddel and methyl as methel (soft 'th' as in weather). At least one listener outside the USA could not distinguish the two words.

Data

Data once meant things known or given that could be used in argument. Readings taken from an apparatus were not yet data. The readings (the raw results) had to be averaged and perhaps worked on in other ways. The data so derived could then be used to support or refute a hypothesis.

It is too late to reclaim the early meaning, but a further change looms – singularization[!]. Data was plural. Many people would keep it so. If you think that way, you may also think that 'the data presented' or 'the given data' is tautological.

Data is pronounced variously [dayta, dahta, datta, dadder], so speak the word clearly. A speaker may say 'Right now we're gunner subject the data to computerization'. During the time it takes us, the bemused foreigners, to interpret the phrase to mean 'We shall now analyze the results', the speaker may utter another sentence which we shall miss.

Evolution of language

Languages evolve; English is a blend of at least three. Slang becomes respectable. We cannot, and should not try to, fix English for ever. But we (all of us) instead of letting English slide aimlessly, should pay attention to the manner in which we let it change. Useful words should be kept alive, including shall, will, results, maize, alternative, lorry (which is more specific than truck). Irregular verbs and irregular plurals could be made regular. [Agendas is on the way 'in'.] A new word might be made for one of the meanings of a word that now has two, e.g. plasma.

M'Fline, were he consulted, would welcome such changes, and others too. He might add 'Why may I not write "two times", sheeps or depend from?'

Too much rigidity would stultify the language, but if we must alter it, let us be sensible about that.

International units of measurement

A professor of linguistics explained that the USA, a 'young' country, innovates fast and that Americans use an existing word in a novel way 'for the sake of change'. If that be so, and if they can initiate the use of 'L' for liter (to avoid confusion over 'l'), why do they resist the adoption of modern weights and measures?

SI units should be used in scientific communication. The symbol μ is a prefix, not a unit; and γ should not be used for μg. Brazilian, Japanese, Hungarian and other scientists have to understand English. Do not add to their burden with gallons or p.s.i. If, for an inscrutable reason, you have to use calories, pounds or °F, give the SI units too. Note that lb is plural as well as singular. If you built apparatus to inches, convert them into mm for description, but do not give a false impression of precision with non-significant digits.

Our obligation to Th. M'Fline

If you think I am unkindly critical, please bear in mind that many people hold similar views and that several of the examples have been provided by editors. We, Americans, British and others, are fortunate in having the International Language as our mother tongue. Let us show our appreciation to M'Fline by restraining abusage and improving good usage.

Chapter Six
Preparation of a doctoral dissertation or thesis

A thesis is an unusually long paper and includes a review, so it resembles a book and is usually divided into chapters. Much of the detail that is described in other chapters herein applies to the writing of a thesis. Although the style should be *concise*, no part should be so *brief* as to risk being inadequate. [The words concise and brief have different meanings but are often confused.]

Specialization

If you have worked mainly on your own, rather than in collaboration with a supervisor, you may have come to know more than anyone else in the world about one narrow subject. So you must explain your problem fully.

Collaboration

Most research is now done by teams. If you worked with others, you must do your utmost to make it clear what parts of the work reported were yours. The examiners (assessors) will be especially curious to know how much you contributed to the thinking, the initiation and the conclusions of joint work. Write about this in a Preface.

Your own work

At the oral examination, the examiners, in asking questions about your interpretations, may be trying to find out whether your thesis was genuinely your own work. At one extreme the supervisor almost writes the thesis. At the other, was the attitude of my supervisor: when I asked whether he would comment on the thesis I had written for a fellowship, he declined on principle and was somewhat shocked at my asking. If you write the thesis entirely yourself, use the same words as you would in deliberate speech; grandiloquent words will do no good. If English is not your first language, and someone helps you with language correction, name him (her) in the Acknowledgements.

Critical evaluation of previous reports

In a thesis, the literature may be more fully reported than in a paper. Even a history of your problem may be acceptable if you can make it interesting. Discuss published work critically but not unkindly. Examiners like to know that you can evaluate other people's reports.

Looking ahead

Your inconclusive experiments may be mentioned and used as a basis for suggestions about what might be done next. Indeed, unlike a scientific paper, a thesis is a suitable place in which to propose experiments to test a hypothesis. [But see Promises, p. 26 (58).] Intelligent speculations, too, may have a place in a thesis. The examiners may even ask you about future aspirations.

Allow enough time for careful correction

If you heed the advice given on p. 2 (When to begin writing), you must start your thesis before you are two-thirds through your course. You may think this is absurd because you have so few results. Even so, you can start on certain parts, as suggested on p. 2. The examiners may be seeking answers to the questions 'Does this student know how to set about a problem? Can he think?' rather than 'Has he done many experiments?'.

Physical presentation of the typescript

When you set out a thesis, consider the reader. Do not merely copy another thesis or offer a collection of assorted preprints and photocopies. If you have already published two or more papers on related subjects, combine them into one narrative for the thesis.

Examine well-printed books and arrange your thesis as a printer would. Write many headings [some people call them captions] and make a clear distinction between different kinds. Copious headings are especially important in the Discussion.

Give a complete Table of Contents (but do not call it an index) and another of figures. Of course, if you *can* supply an Index, that would be impressive, but there is rarely time.

Place the Summary before the Introduction.

Several small tables are better than a few large ones. Place them, and the diagrams, near the relevant text; the smaller the table the easier this becomes. Arrange tables, diagrams and pictures upright (portrait fashion); readers dislike having to turn books sideways to study 'landscapes'.

Attend to the recommendations in Chapter Two. Examiners who find sloppy presentation may suspect that the experiments were sloppy too. Leave ample margins, with that at the foot greater than that at the top. A scanty bottom margin makes the typescript seem to be sliding off the paper. If the paper is size A4 and the sheets are stab bound (stapled through the margin), the typescript should be no wider than 140 mm; a wide left margin is essential. If the bound volume will be cumbersome and thick, perhaps you should make two volumes. If, for this or any other reason, your thesis is in two volumes, make it clear that this is so, both on the cover and on the title page. The two assessors of one Ph.D. student each examined a different volume without realizing there was another.

You should correct the script yourself

Every research student should read Clark (1960) on preparing for research. The prose is a joy to read. Unfortunately, the book may be difficult to find.

Various books have been published on thesis writing. A good essay is that by Hawkins (1982). He warns that an assessor may check some of the references for accuracy. He writes about 'errors that have occurred'. The errors include: misquotations; tables upside-down; bad captions; masses of complicated data with no explanation; statistics that make no sense; incorrect references; words left out; and literal errors. So be painstaking over the preparation, reporting of results, spelling and punctuation; there will be neither editor nor printer to put those in order for you.

One often finds the standard error of the mean confused with the the stand deviation. So never omit the M from S.E.M.

Did you find the two errors in the paragraph above? If not, look again; then let that be an example to show how carefully one must correct a script.

If the examiners find faulty logic, they will tell you, even if it is as trivial as 'The patient had anaemia because I observed a low haematocrit'.

Do not be discouraged

Are you overwhelmed by all the details that need your attention? I hope
not. Attending to details takes time, which may prevent your doing all
the experiments you would like to do. May I remind you that

'A good thesis based on few results
betters a bad one based on many'?

Even though they point out errors, the examiners are probably
sympathetic. They will not fail you for a few small faults if they are
convinced that you are a good researcher and that you are able to
communicate.

Chapter Seven
Bibliography

References

Baer, D. M. (1983). Adjectives, nouns, and hyphens. *Science* **222**, 368.

(1) Booth, V. H. (1960). Legibility of print. *Research* **9**, 2–5.

Clark, G. Kitson (1960). *Guide for Research Students Working on Historical Subjects.* Cambridge University Press.

de Bono, E. (1967). *The Use of Lateral Thinking.* Pelican Books, Harmondsworth, UK.

Dixon, H. B. F. (1983). Return of the dalton. *Trends in Biochemical Science* **8**, 49.

Hartree, E. F. (1976). Ethics for authors: a case history of acrosin. *Perspectives in Biology & Medicine* **20**, 82–92.

Hawkins, C. (1982). Write the MD thesis. In *How to Do It*, pp. 52–61. British Medical Association, London. See B (7).

Hers, H-G. (1984). Making science a good read. *Nature* **307**, 205.

Hildebrand, M. (1983). Noun use criticism. *Science* **221**, 698.

Holman, E. (1962). Concerning more effective medical writing. A plea for sobriety, accuracy and brevity in medical writing. *Journal of the American Medical Association* **181**, 245–7.

Kenny, P. (1983). *Public Speaking for Scientists and Engineers.* Hilger, Bristol.

Mackay, A. L. (1977). *Harvest of a Quiet Eye.* Institute of Physics, Bristol.

Maier, N. R. F. (1933). An aspect of human reasoning. *British Journal of Psychology* **24**, 144–55.

Norman, P. (1980). *Sunday Times Magazine* 1980-03-02.

Norris, J. R. (1978). How to give a research talk: notes for inexperienced lecturers. *Biologist* **25**, 68–74.

Perttunen, J. M. (1975). The English sentence. *Luonnon Tutkija* **79**, 113–17.

Roland, C. G. (1976). Thoughts about medical writing. XXXVII. Verify your reference. *Anesthesia & Analgesia... Current Researches* **55**, 717–18.

Strunk, W. (1959). *The Elements of Style* (various editions, e.g. with E. B. White). Macmillan, New York.

Woodford, F. P. (1970). Editor, *Scientific Writing for Graduate Students*. Macmillan, New York & London.

Instructions to authors

Many journals issue Directives to authors. A good example is the
(2) *Biochemical Journal's Instructions to Authors*, which includes a piece on Policy, a useful list of abbreviations, symbols, etc. and a reminder to write RNAase and DNAase. Obtain the booklet from the Biochemical Society (7 Warwick Court, London WC1R 5DP).

If you have not seen a questionnaire that editors send to referees, try to obtain one. Then ensure that your paper would elicit satisfactory answers before you submit it.

Books on scientific writing

(3) *Writing Scientific Papers in English*, by M. O'Connor & F. P. Woodford (1979), Pitman, Tunbridge Wells, UK, is one of the best books on scientific writing.

(4)   K. W. Houp & T. E. Pearsall (1977), in their *Reporting Technical Information*, Glencoe Press, New York, and Collier–Macmillan, London, have an entertaining chapter on writing in clear English.

(5)   *Scientists Must Write: A Guide to Better Writing for Scientists, Engineers and Students*, by Robert Barrass (1983), Chapman & Hall, London, includes a section on reading the literature, which is unusual.

(6)   *How to Write and Publish a Scientific Paper*, by Robert A. Day (1983), ISI Press, Philadelphia, gives a wealth of advice on how to write so that your paper will be accepted for publication.

A Manual of Style, University of Chicago Press, is one of the best-known style books in the USA.

(7)   *How to Do It* (1982), British Medical Association, London, is the most versatile of these books. Written by medical doctors, the essays tell how to write, to speak, to chair a conference, to attract a reader, to referee a paper, to be a dictator, to examine, to be examined, to use a library and to perform two dozen other activities.

How to Write and Publish Papers in the Medical Sciences, by E. J. Huth (1982), ISI Press, Philadelphia, includes a piece on ethics.

Some of the books published abroad are expensive.

English usage

(8) H. W. Fowler's *Modern English Usage*, as edited by E. Gowers, Oxford
(9) University Press, or by M. Nicholson (as *American–English Usage*,

Oxford University Press Inc., New York), is invaluable. The Nicholson edition is out-of-print but well worth seeking.

E. Partridge's *Usage and Abusage: a Guide to Good English* (1982), Hamilton, London, is preferred to Fowler by some editors.

Some passages in each of these books are slowly becoming outmoded.

(10) *Everyman's Good English Guide* by Harry Fieldhouse (1982), Dent, London, is more contemporary than the other works, but not so extensive. The book gives help on many troublesome words and recommends pronunciation. The grammatical section is easily readable.

Another helpful book is E. S. C. Weiner's (1983) *The Oxford Guide to English Usage*, Oxford University Press. This book includes a Glossary of 'troublesome' words.

(11) *What a Word!* by A. P. Herbert (1935), Methuen, London, who calls
(12) you Bobby, shows that good style need not be dull. B. Dixon (1973) in *Sciwrite* (*Chemistry in Britain* **9**, 70–2) urges lively writing and gives examples of stuffiness.

Books for editors

(13) *Copy-Editing* by J. Butcher (1983), Cambridge University Press, contains a great amount of information, some of which cannot easily be found elsewhere. The book describes the astonishing amount and variety of work that has to be done on a script and its illustrations between its receipt by the publisher and touching of the first key by the typesetter. Printing techniques have changed so much recently, however, that the book is not up to date in all respects.

(14) *Editing Scientific Books and Journals* by Maeve O'Connor (1978), Pitman, Tunbridge Wells, is excellent; every editor should have this book.

The Oxford Dictionary for Writers and Editors, Clarendon Press, Oxford, helps with many problems of detail (capitals, spelling, abbreviations, confusables...) that only specialists can remember in total.

The British Standards Institution (2 Park St, London W1A 2BS) has issued various standards of interest to scientists and editors, e.g. BS5261 (1976) on *Copy Marking & Proof Correcting*.

Dictionaries

(15) The *Concise Oxford Dictionary*, Oxford University Press, and *Chambers Twentieth Century Dictionary*, Chambers, Edinburgh, are admirable.

(16) For American meanings or spellings that are sometimes different from European, consult, for example, *Webster's New Collegiate Dictionary of*

the English Language, Merriam, Springfield, Mass., or the *Concise Oxford Dictionary*.

There are many other dictionaries. Olive Holmes (1980) (*Scholarly Publishing*, **11**, 229) gives a usefully annotated list of dictionaries. Unfortunately, her review was published a few months ahead of dictionaries by Collins, London, and by Longman, London.

(17)   *Roget's Thesaurus* is invaluable in helping one to find a word. Several editions are available. Differently arranged is *Collins New World Thesaurus* by C. Laird (1979), Collins, London & Glasgow.

Every scientist should have a dictionary of science. Here are three. *Dictionary of Science & Technology* (1983), Chambers, Edinburgh. *Longman Dictionary of Scientific Usage* by A. Goodman & E. M. F. Payne (1980), Longman, London. *A Dictionary of Science* by E. B. Uvarov, D. R. Chapman & A. Isaacs (1982), Penguin, Harmondsworth, UK.

There are other science dictionaries. To test a dictionary, look up items in your field. If the spellings or explanations are out of date, beware!

More a book to be read than consulted as a dictionary is *Words of Science* by Isaac Asimov (1974), Harrap, London.

Units and nomenclature

Several books have been published on SI units, including the following.
Manual of Symbols & Terminology for Physicochemical Quantities & Units, Pergamon, Oxford. This has been published in *Pure & Applied Chemistry* (1979) **51**, 1–14.

(18)   *Quantities, Units, and Symbols* by the Symbols Committee (1975), The Royal Society, London.

A Dictionary of Scientific Units, by H. G. Jarrard & D. B. McNeill (1980), Chapman & Hall, London.

SI: The International System of Units, by D. T. Goldman & R. J. Bell (1981), HMSO, London.

A beautiful chart, *Quantities & SI Units*, is printed in seven colours and published by Nederlands Normalisatie-instituut, Polakweg 5, Rijswijk ZH, Netherlands.

If you have difficulty in understanding a unit as defined in one book [many of us do] try reading about the unit in a different sort of book, for example a science dictionary.

(19)   BS3763 (1976) on *SI Units* and BS4795 (1972) on *All-Numeric Dates* are issued by The British Standards Institution, 2 Park St, London W1A 2BS.

Rules for nomenclature of chemicals are given in *Nomenclature of*

Inorganic Chemistry by IUPAC (International Union of Pure & Applied Chemistry) (1971), Butterworths, London, and *Nomenclature of Organic Chemistry* (1979), Pergamon, Oxford. Nearly all the information in the latter is in *Biochemical Nomenclature & Related Documents* (1978), Biochemical Society, London & Colchester, and the price is much lower.

For a quick check on spelling of chemical names you may consult a well-produced catalogue of chemicals. Such catalogues include those of
(20) Koch–Light Laboratories Ltd, Colnbrook, Bucks SL3 0BZ, and BDH Chemicals Ltd, Poole, Dorset BH12 4NN.

Date of printing

The dates given for the books are the dates of issue. A date may be that of a reprinting of an older edition.

Index

Suffixes *a,b,c* refer to top, middle and lowest thirds of a page, respectively.